# THE MACHINES™

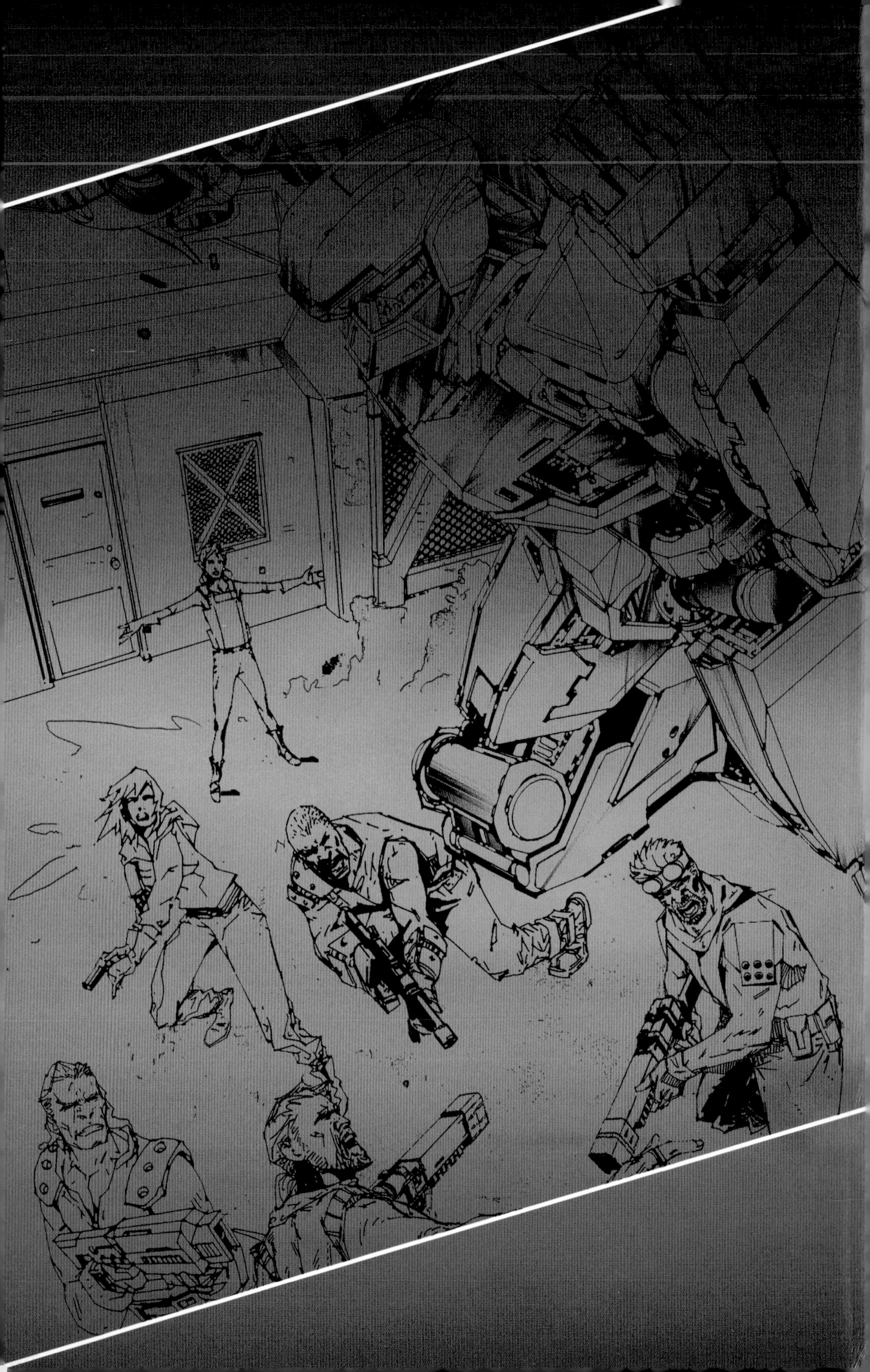

# THE MACHINES™

**SCRIPT**
**JOHN McLEAN-FOREMAN**

**ART**
**ERIC NGUYEN**

**COLORS**
**MICHAEL ATIYEH**

**LETTERS**
**MICHAEL HEISLER**

**COVER ART**
**WILLIAM CHEN**

**Directive**
GAMES

**DARK HORSE BOOKS**

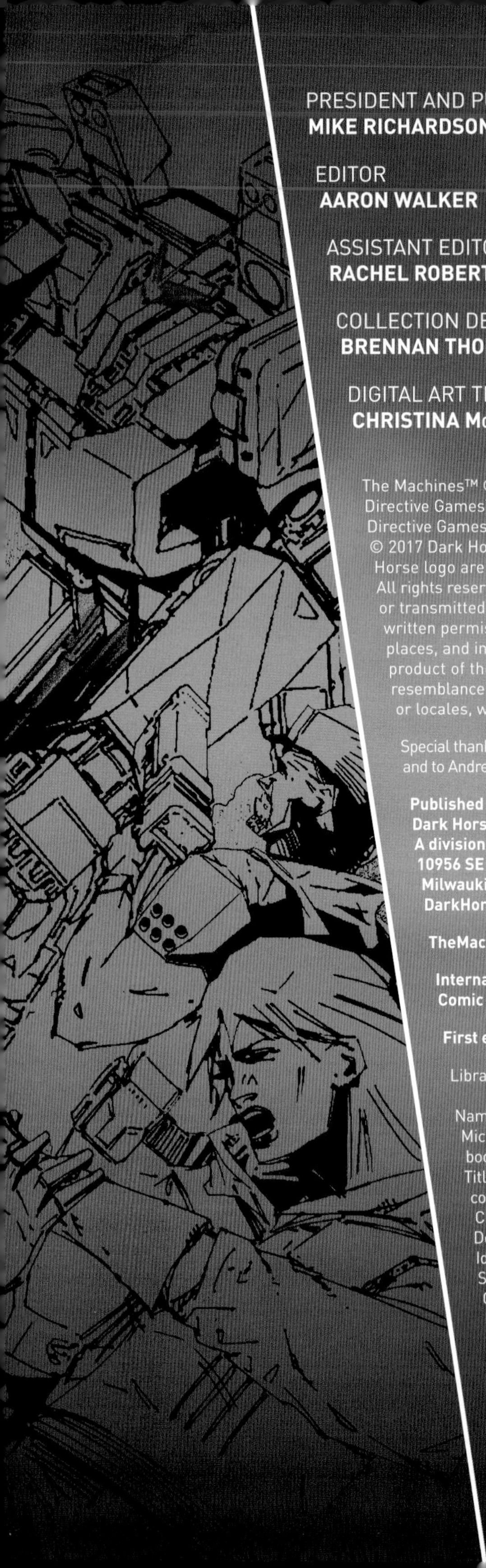

PRESIDENT AND PUBLISHER
**MIKE RICHARDSON**

EDITOR
**AARON WALKER**

ASSISTANT EDITOR
**RACHEL ROBERTS**

COLLECTION DESIGNER
**BRENNAN THOME**

DIGITAL ART TECHNICIAN
**CHRISTINA McKENZIE**



Special thanks to Atli Mar Sveinsson at Directive Games, and to Andrea Sanders and Kari Yadro at Dark Horse Comics.

**Published by**
**Dark Horse Books**
**A division of Dark Horse Comics, Inc.**
**10956 SE Main Street**
**Milwaukie, OR 97222**
**DarkHorse.com**

**TheMachinesGame.com**

**International Licensing: (503) 905-2377**
**Comic Shop Locator Service: (888) 266-4226**

**First edition: February 2017**

Library of Congress Cataloging-in-Publication Data

Names: McLean-Foreman, John, author. | Nguyen, Eric, artist. | Atiyeh, Michael, colorist. | Heisler, Michael, letterer. | Chen, William (Comic book artist), artist.
Title: The machines / script, John McLean-Foreman ; art, Eric Nguyen ; colors, Michael Atiyeh ; lettering, Michael Heisler ; cover art, William Chen.
Description: First edition. | Milwaukie, OR : Dark Horse Books, 2017.
Identifiers: LCCN 2016034676 | ISBN 9781506700519 (hardback)
Subjects: LCSH: Comic books, strips, etc. | BISAC: GAMES / Video & Electronic.
Classification: LCC PN6728.M326 M35 2017 | DDC 741.5/973--dc23
LC record available at https://lccn.loc.gov/2016034676

**ISBN 978-1-50670-051-9**

**10 9 8 7 6 5 4 3 2 1**
**Printed in China**

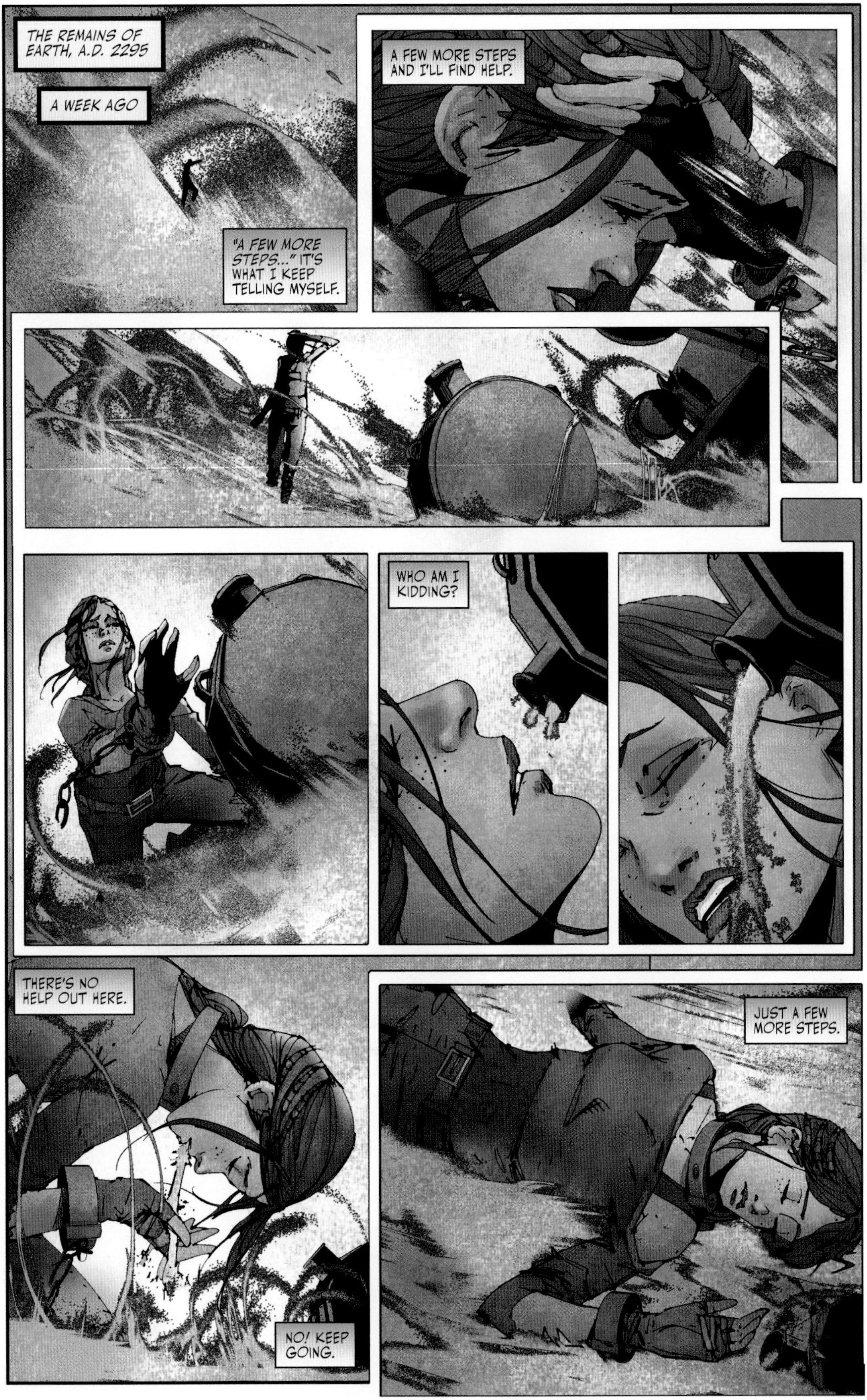

THE REMAINS OF EARTH, A.D. 2295
A WEEK AGO
"A FEW MORE STEPS..." IT'S WHAT I KEEP TELLING MYSELF.
A FEW MORE STEPS AND I'LL FIND HELP.
WHO AM I KIDDING?
THERE'S NO HELP OUT HERE.
NO! KEEP GOING.
JUST A FEW MORE STEPS.

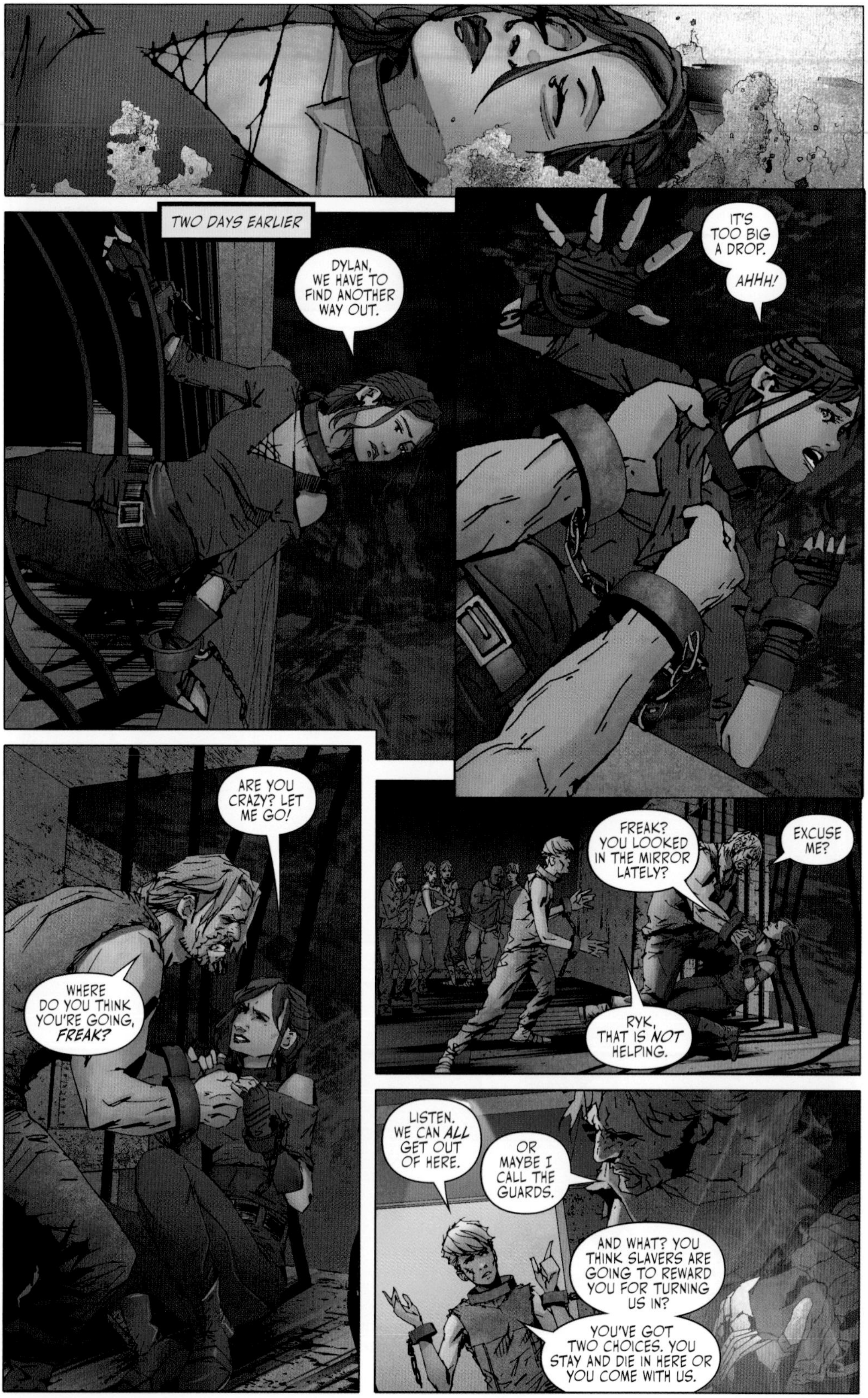

TWO DAYS EARLIER
DYLAN, WE HAVE TO FIND ANOTHER WAY OUT.
IT'S TOO BIG A DROP.
AHHH!
ARE YOU CRAZY? LET ME GO!
WHERE DO YOU THINK YOU'RE GOING, *FREAK?*
FREAK? YOU LOOKED IN THE MIRROR LATELY?
EXCUSE ME?
RYK, THAT IS *NOT* HELPING.
LISTEN. WE CAN *ALL* GET OUT OF HERE.
OR MAYBE I CALL THE GUARDS.
AND WHAT? YOU THINK SLAVERS ARE GOING TO REWARD YOU FOR TURNING US IN?
YOU'VE GOT TWO CHOICES. YOU STAY AND DIE IN HERE OR YOU COME WITH US.

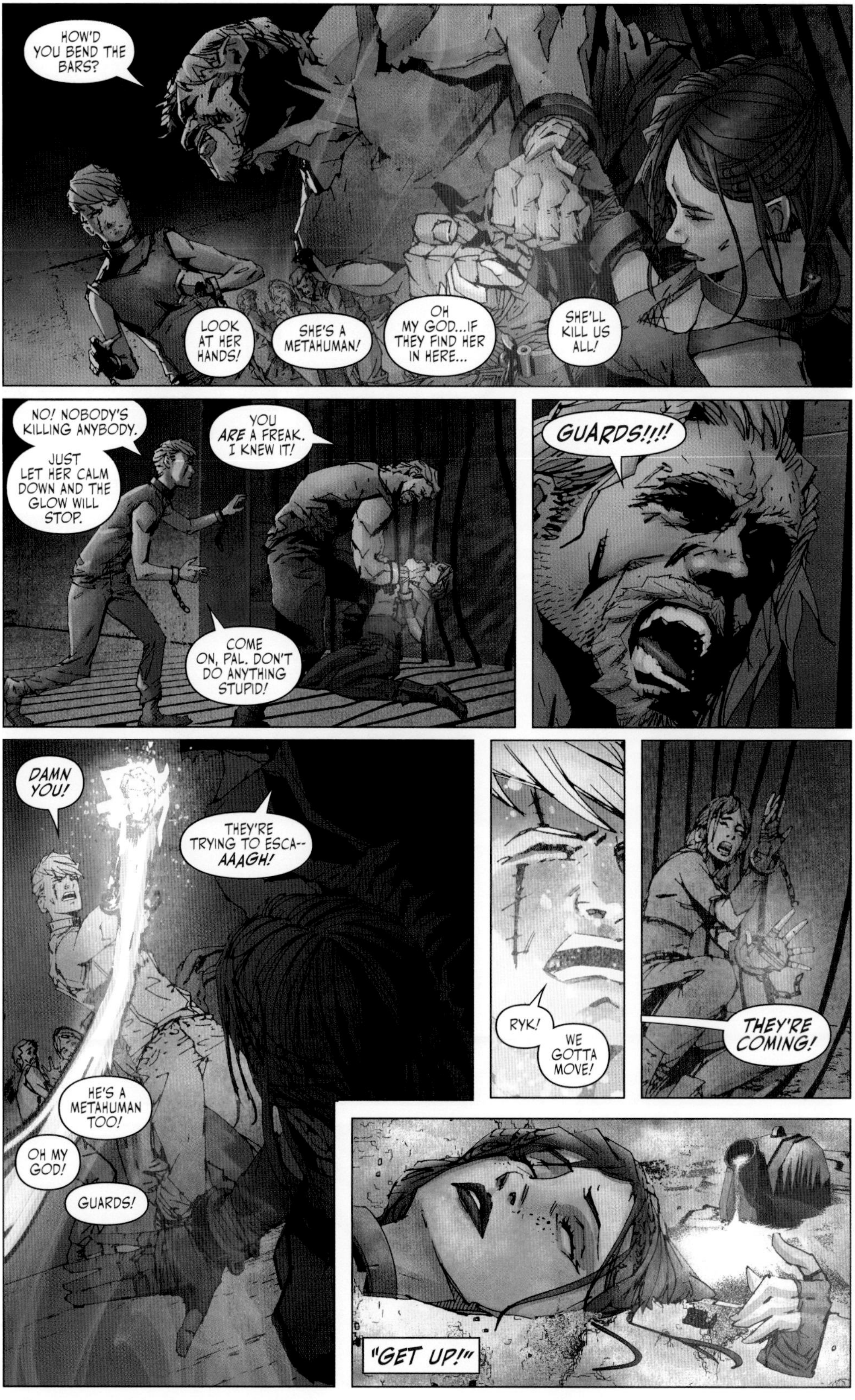
HOW'D YOU BEND THE BARS?
LOOK AT HER HANDS!
SHE'S A METAHUMAN!
OH MY GOD...IF THEY FIND HER IN HERE...
SHE'LL KILL US ALL!
NO! NOBODY'S KILLING ANYBODY.
JUST LET HER CALM DOWN AND THE GLOW WILL STOP.
YOU *ARE* A FREAK. I KNEW IT!
COME ON, PAL. DON'T DO ANYTHING STUPID!
GUARDS!!!!
DAMN YOU!
THEY'RE TRYING TO ESCA-- *AAAGH!*
HE'S A METAHUMAN TOO!
OH MY GOD!
GUARDS!
RYK!
WE GOTTA MOVE!
THEY'RE COMING!
"GET UP!"

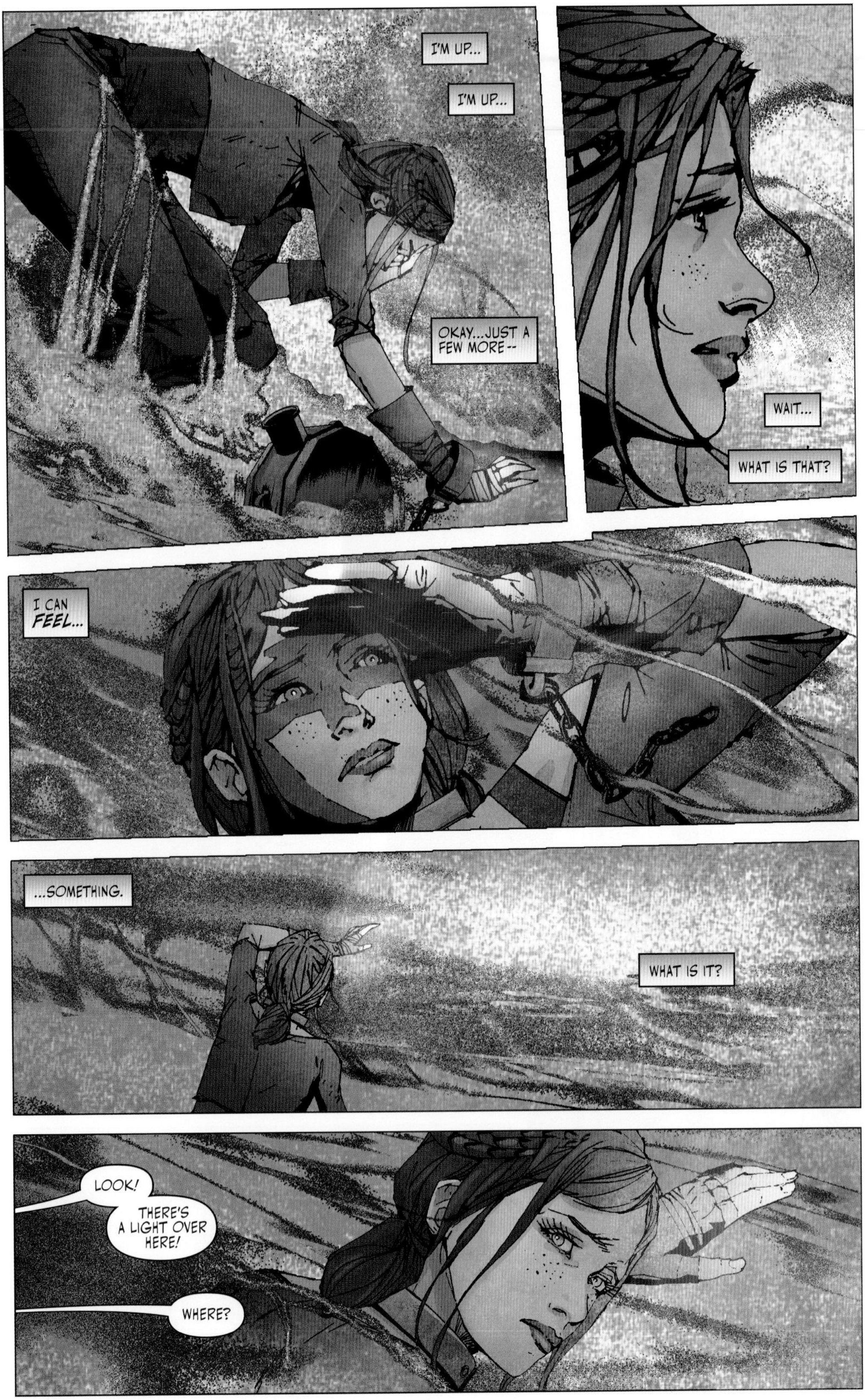
I'M UP...
I'M UP...
OKAY...JUST A FEW MORE--
WAIT...
WHAT IS THAT?
I CAN FEEL...
...SOMETHING.
WHAT IS IT?
LOOK!
THERE'S A LIGHT OVER HERE!
WHERE?

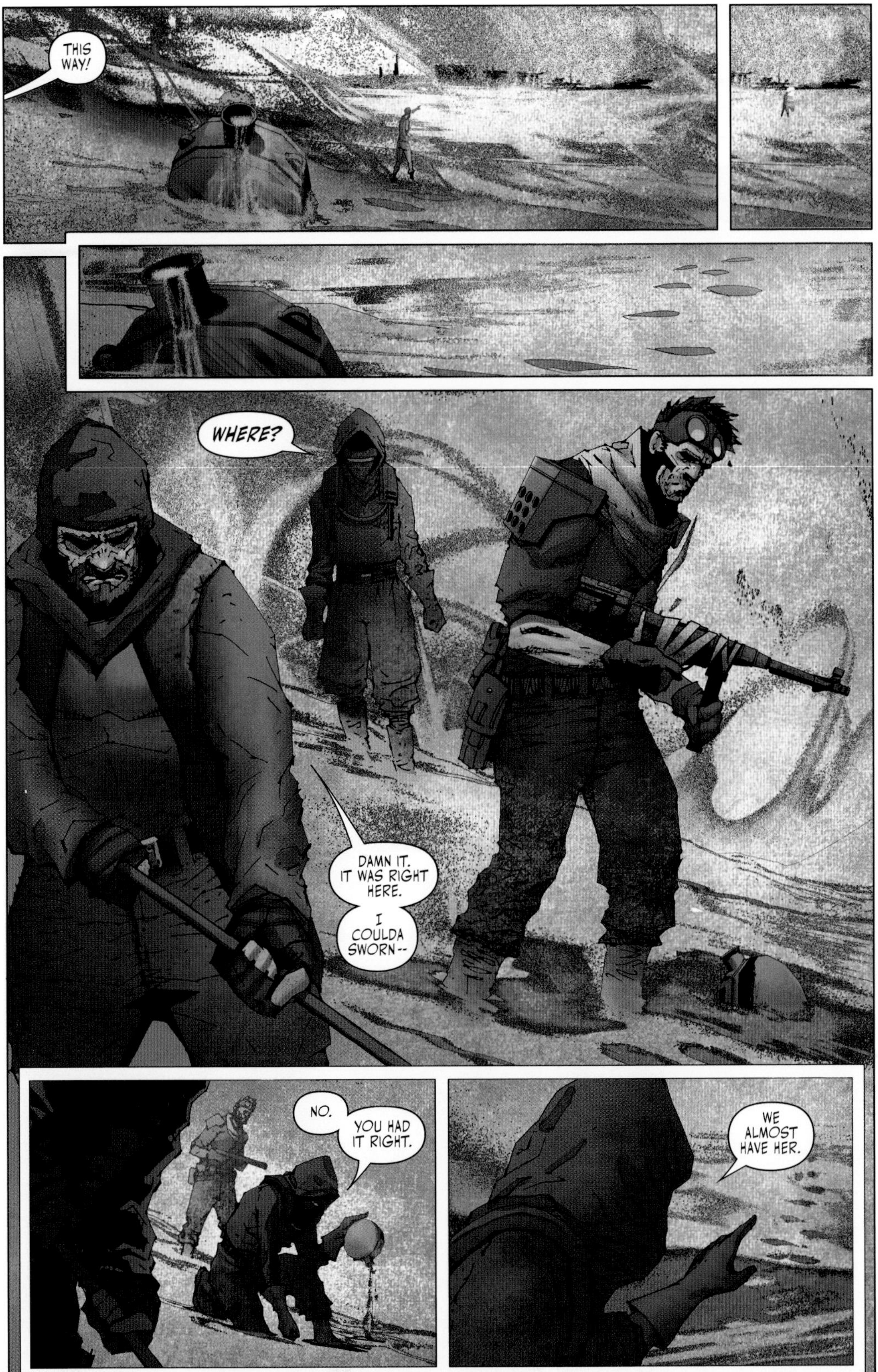
THIS WAY!
WHERE?
DAMN IT. IT WAS RIGHT HERE.
I COULDA SWORN--
NO.
YOU HAD IT RIGHT.
WE ALMOST HAVE HER.

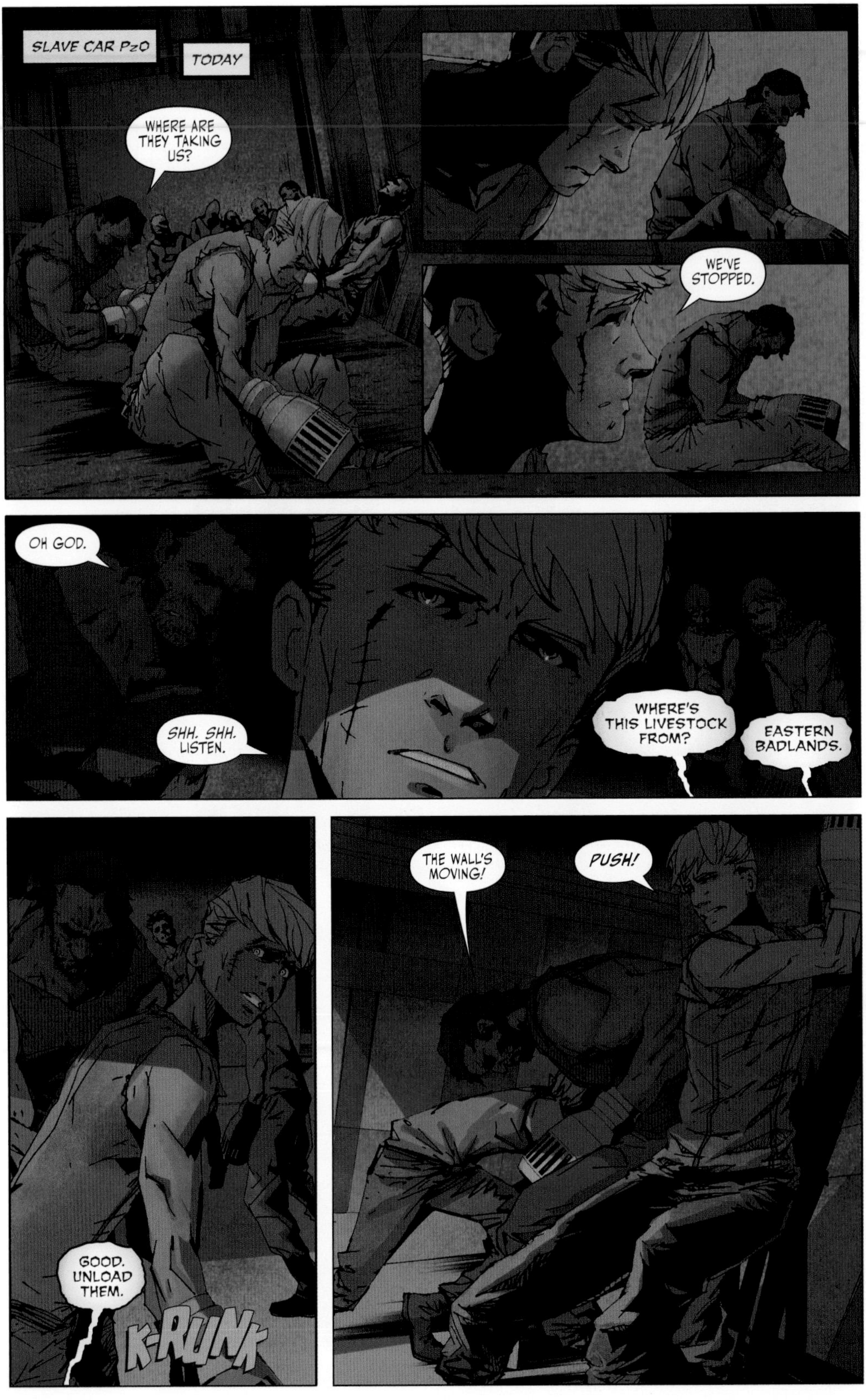
SLAVE CAR PzO
TODAY
WHERE ARE THEY TAKING US?
WE'VE STOPPED.
OH GOD.
SHH. SHH. LISTEN.
WHERE'S THIS LIVESTOCK FROM?
EASTERN BADLANDS.
GOOD. UNLOAD THEM.
K-RUNK
THE WALL'S MOVING!
PUSH!

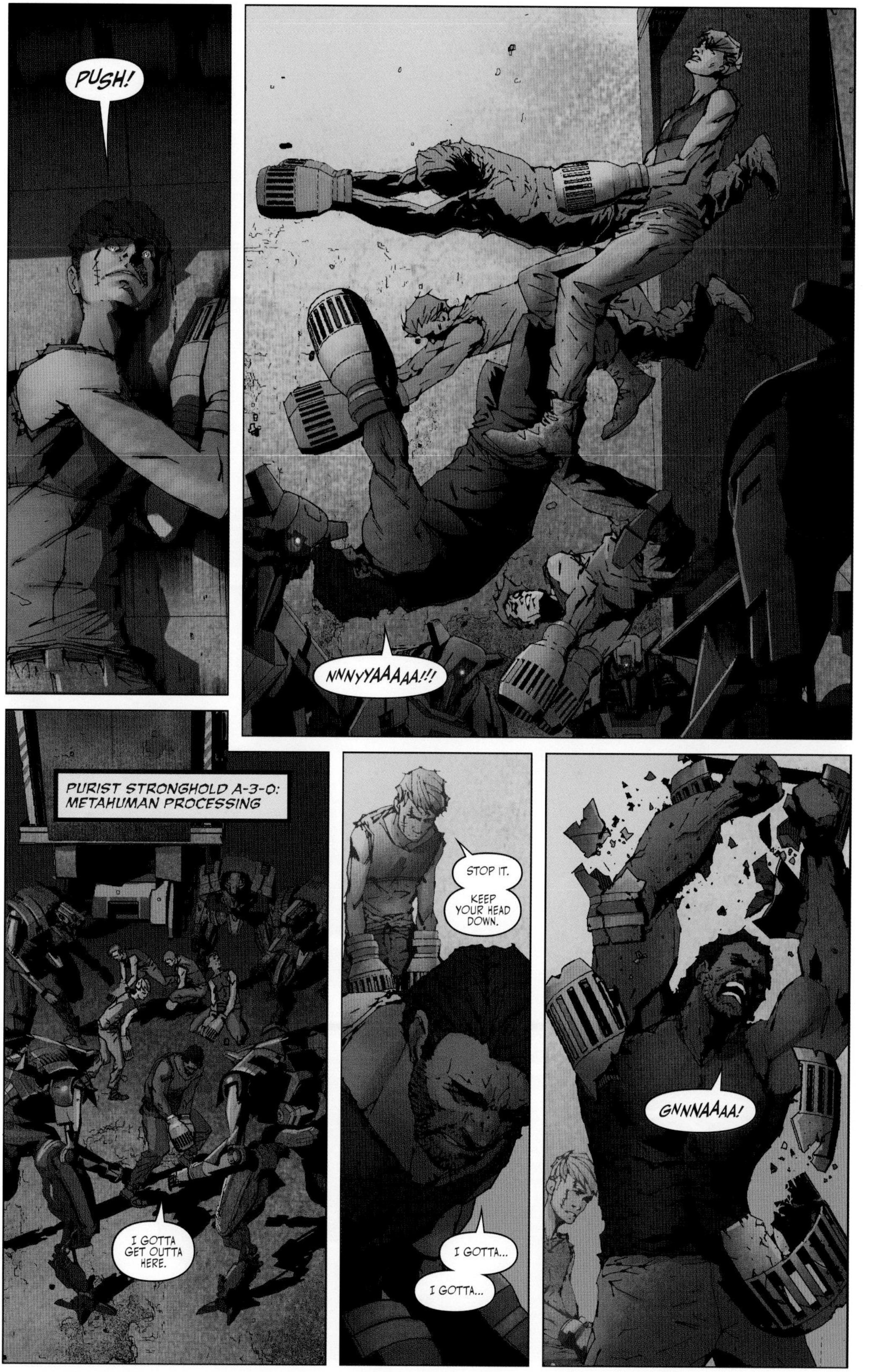
PUSH!
NNNyYAAAAA!!!
PURIST STRONGHOLD A-3-0: METAHUMAN PROCESSING
I GOTTA GET OUTTA HERE.
STOP IT.
KEEP YOUR HEAD DOWN.
I GOTTA...
I GOTTA...
GNNAAAA!

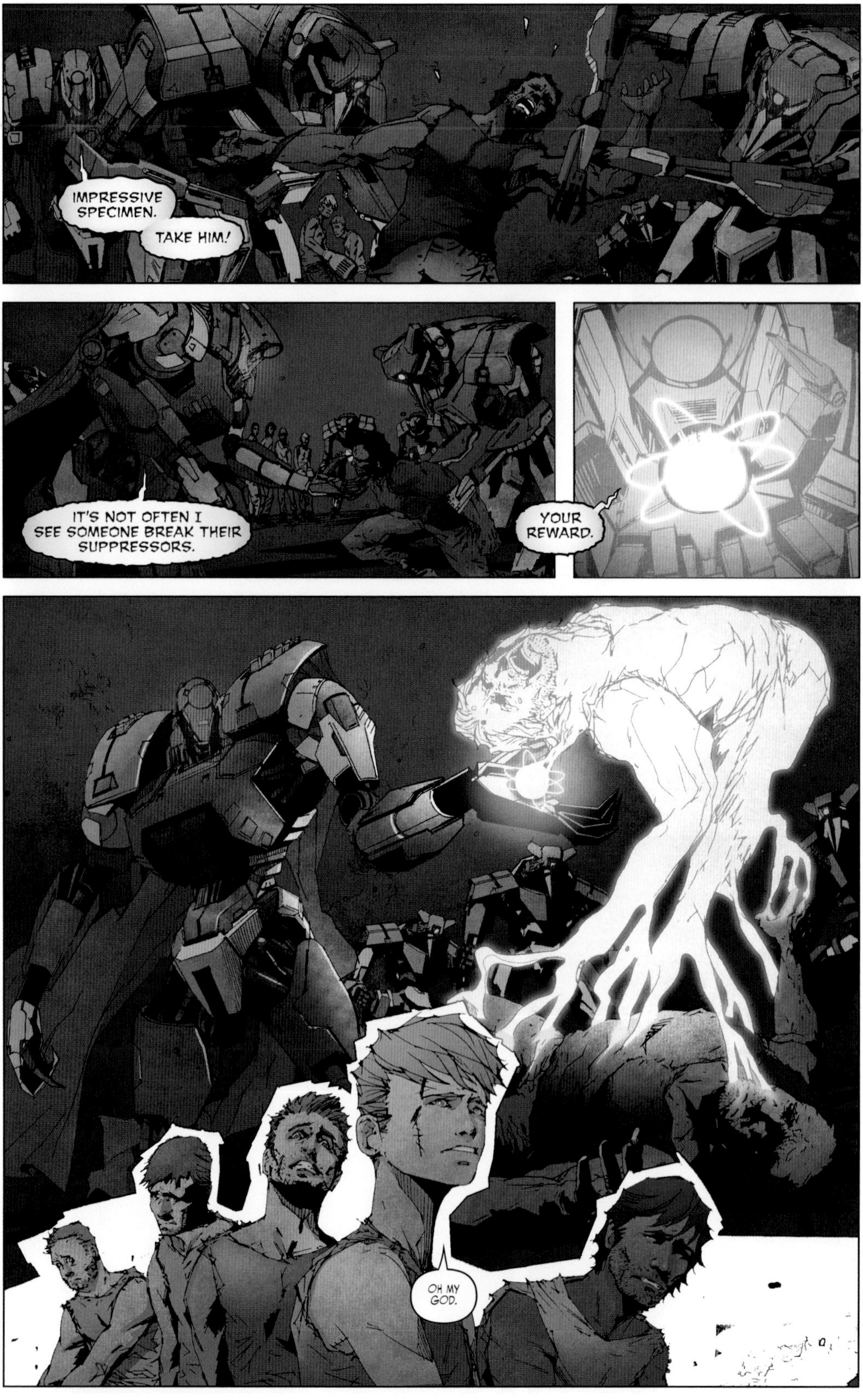
IMPRESSIVE SPECIMEN.
TAKE HIM!
IT'S NOT OFTEN I SEE SOMEONE BREAK THEIR SUPPRESSORS.
YOUR REWARD.
OH MY GOD.

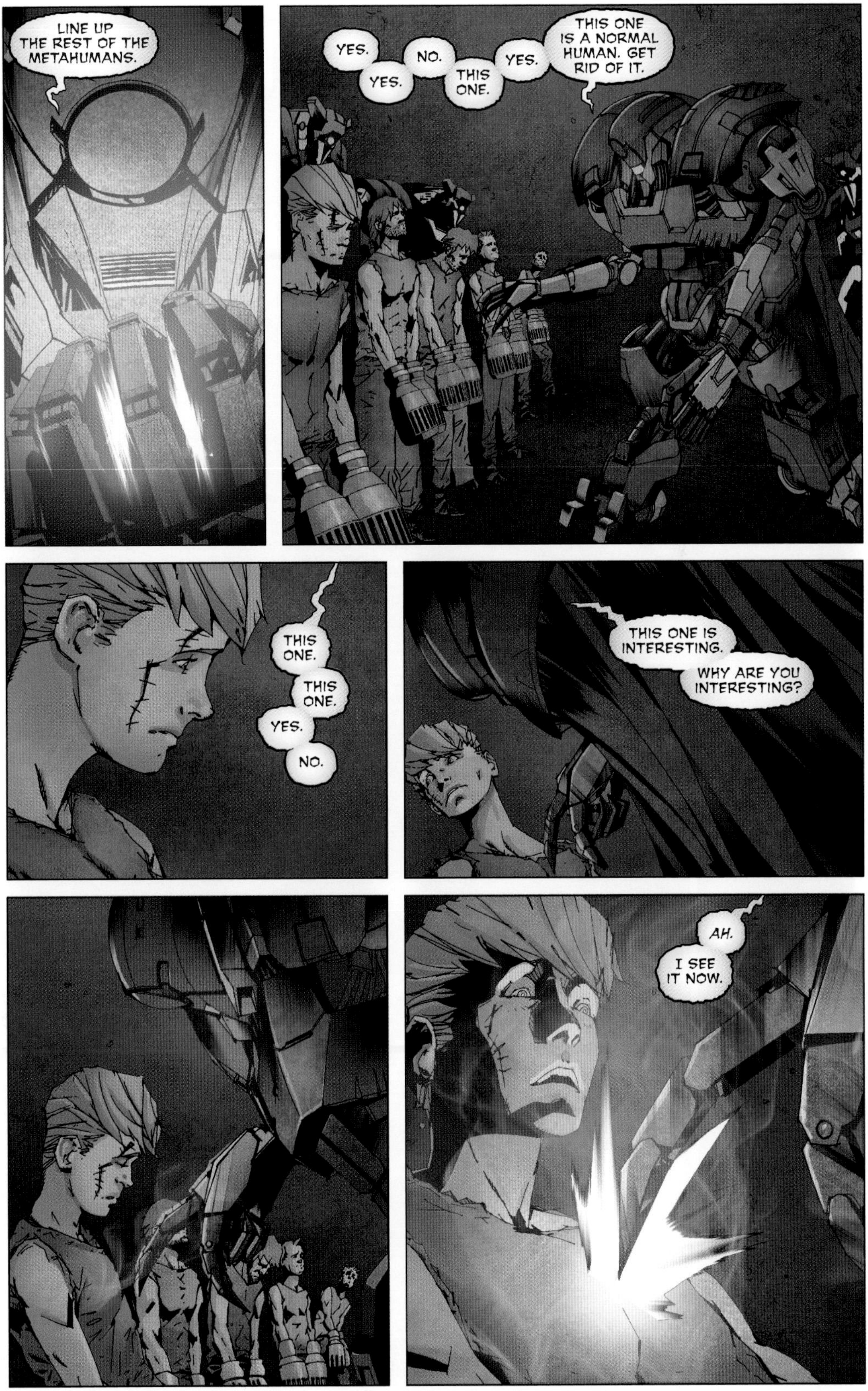
LINE UP THE REST OF THE METAHUMANS.
YES.
YES.
NO.
THIS ONE.
YES.
THIS ONE IS A NORMAL HUMAN. GET RID OF IT.
THIS ONE.
THIS ONE.
YES.
NO.
THIS ONE IS INTERESTING.
WHY ARE YOU INTERESTING?
AH.
I SEE IT NOW.

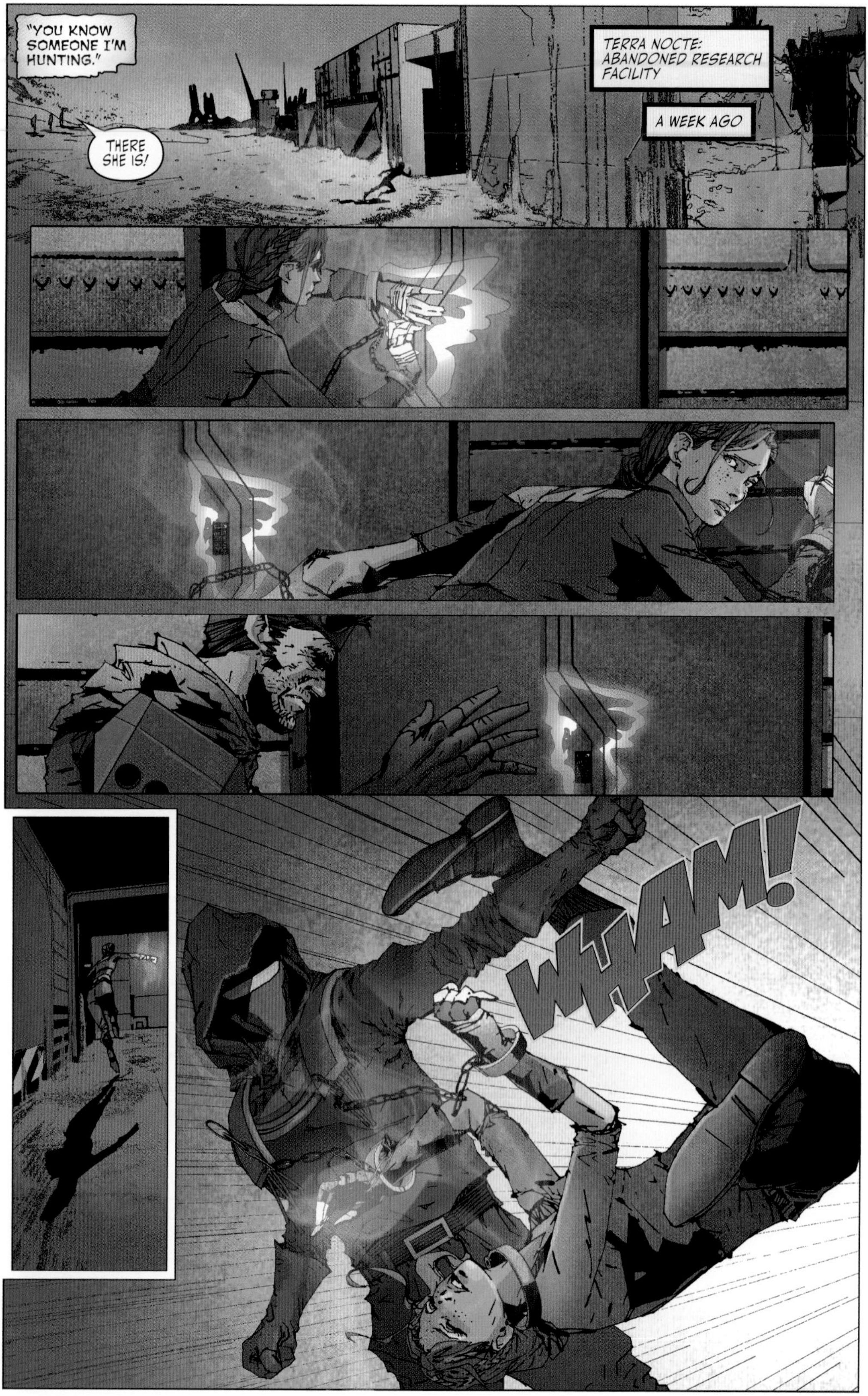
"YOU KNOW SOMEONE I'M HUNTING."
TERRA NOCTE: ABANDONED RESEARCH FACILITY
A WEEK AGO
THERE SHE IS!
WHAM!

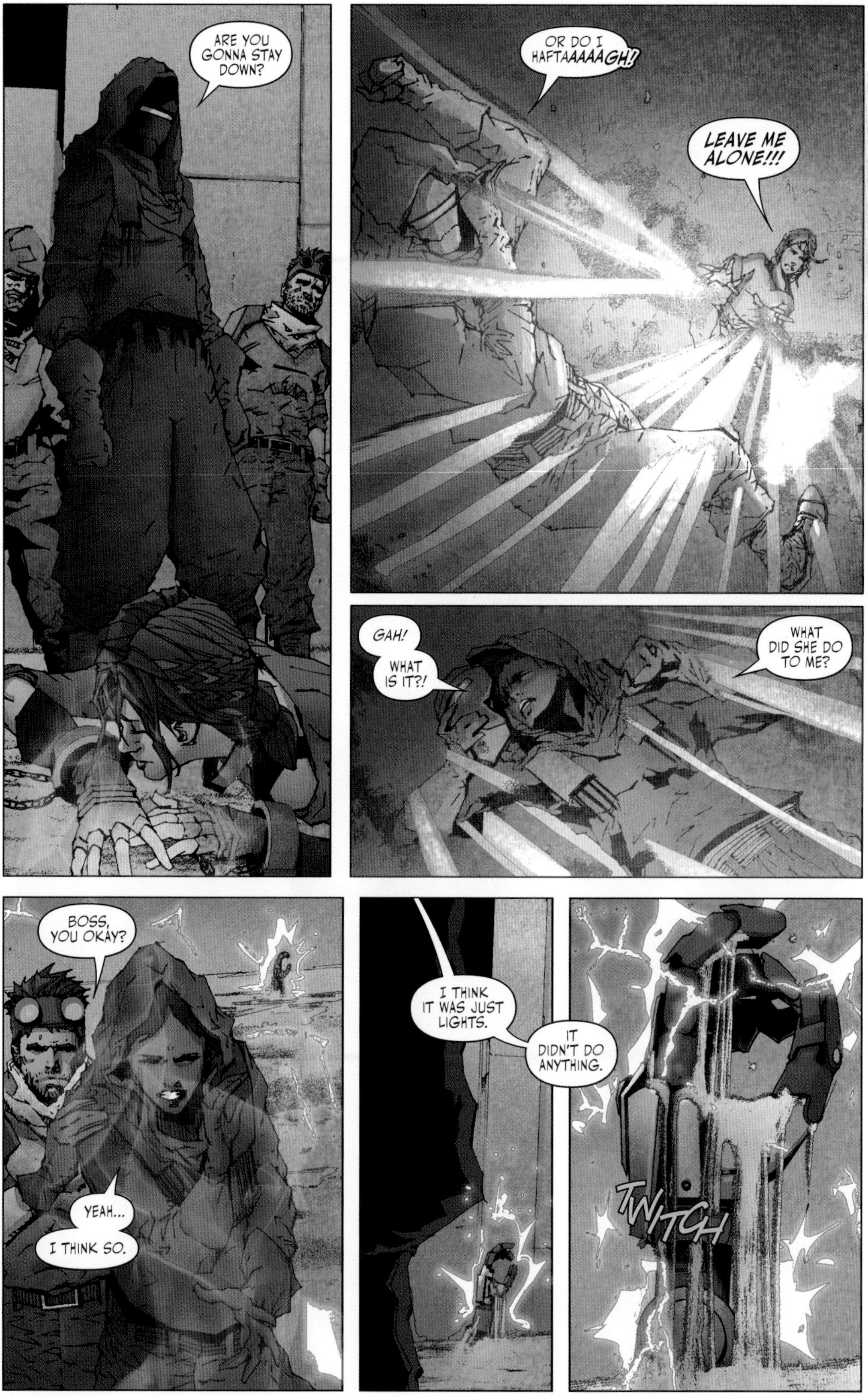
ARE YOU GONNA STAY DOWN?
OR DO I HAFTAAAAAGH!
LEAVE ME ALONE!!!
GAH!
WHAT IS IT?!
WHAT DID SHE DO TO ME?
BOSS, YOU OKAY?
YEAH...
I THINK SO.
I THINK IT WAS JUST LIGHTS.
IT DIDN'T DO ANYTHING.
TWITCH

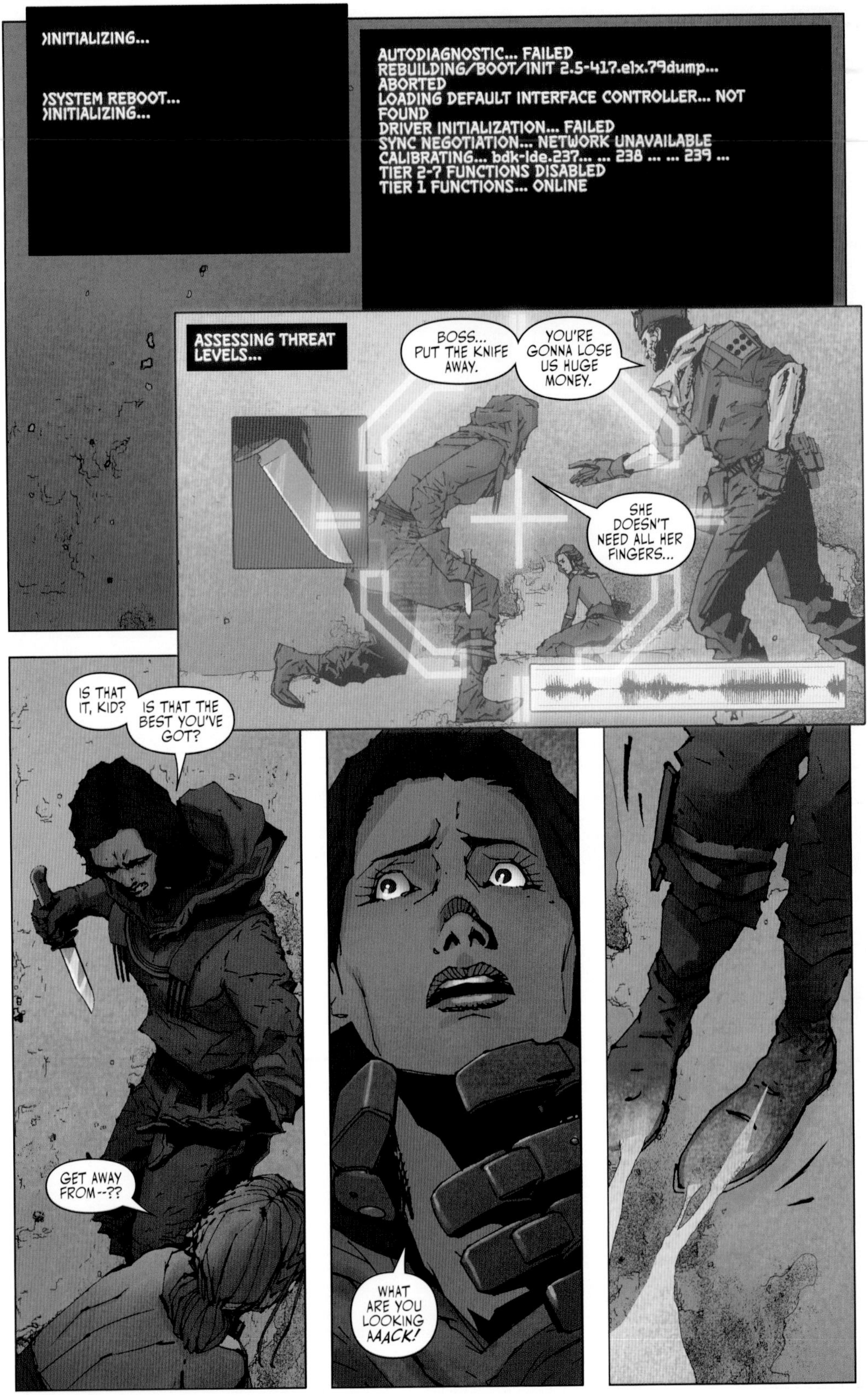

›INITIALIZING...
›SYSTEM REBOOT...
›INITIALIZING...
AUTODIAGNOSTIC... FAILED
REBUILDING/BOOT/INIT 2.5-417.elx.79dump...
ABORTED
LOADING DEFAULT INTERFACE CONTROLLER... NOT FOUND
DRIVER INITIALIZATION... FAILED
SYNC NEGOTIATION... NETWORK UNAVAILABLE
CALIBRATING... bdk-lde.237... ... 238 ... ... 239 ...
TIER 2-7 FUNCTIONS DISABLED
TIER 1 FUNCTIONS... ONLINE
ASSESSING THREAT LEVELS...
BOSS... PUT THE KNIFE AWAY.
YOU'RE GONNA LOSE US HUGE MONEY.
SHE DOESN'T NEED ALL HER FINGERS...
IS THAT IT, KID?
IS THAT THE BEST YOU'VE GOT?
GET AWAY FROM--??
WHAT ARE YOU LOOKING AAACK!

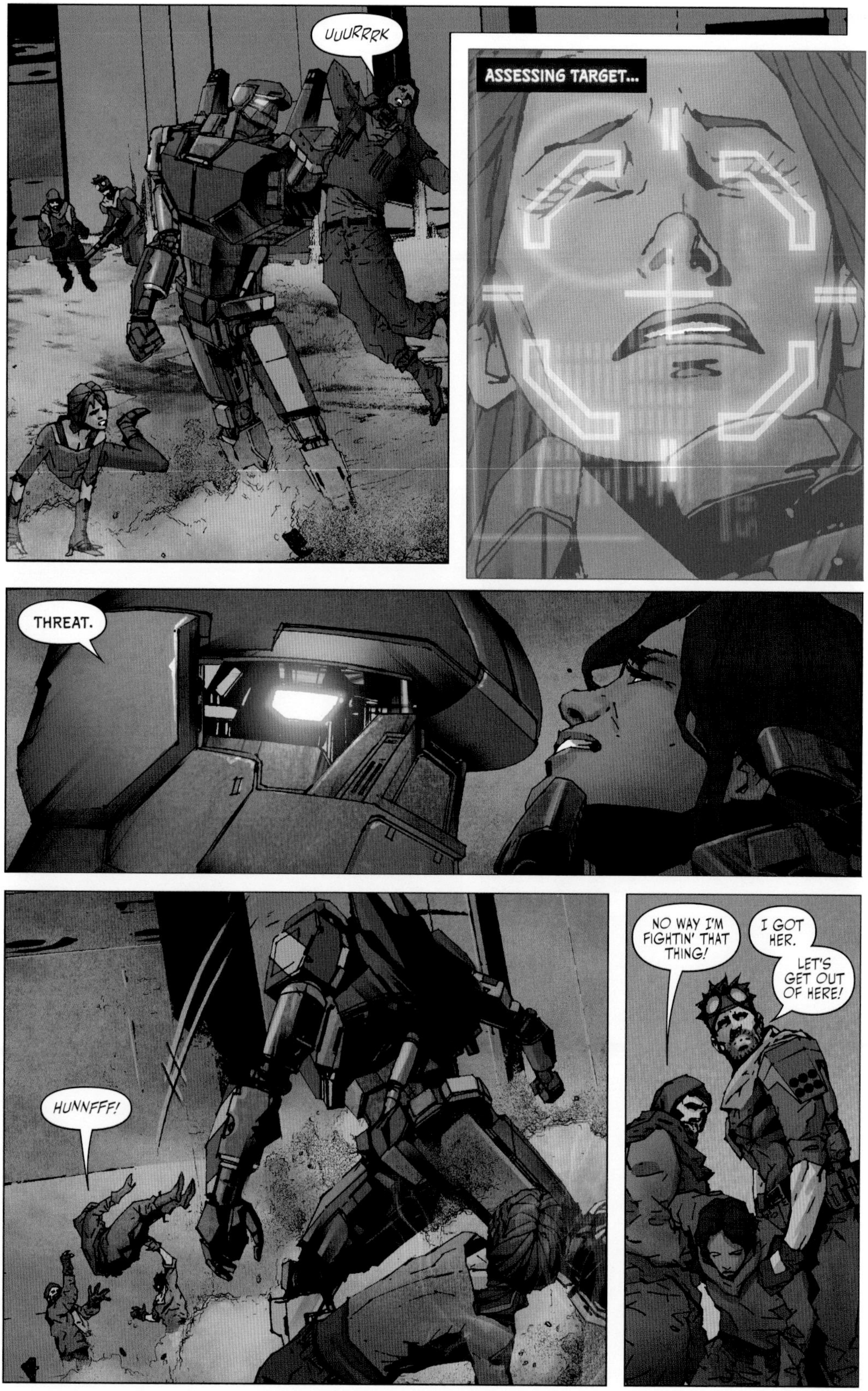
UUURRRK
ASSESSING TARGET...
THREAT.
HUNNFFF!
NO WAY I'M FIGHTIN' THAT THING!
I GOT HER.
LET'S GET OUT OF HERE!

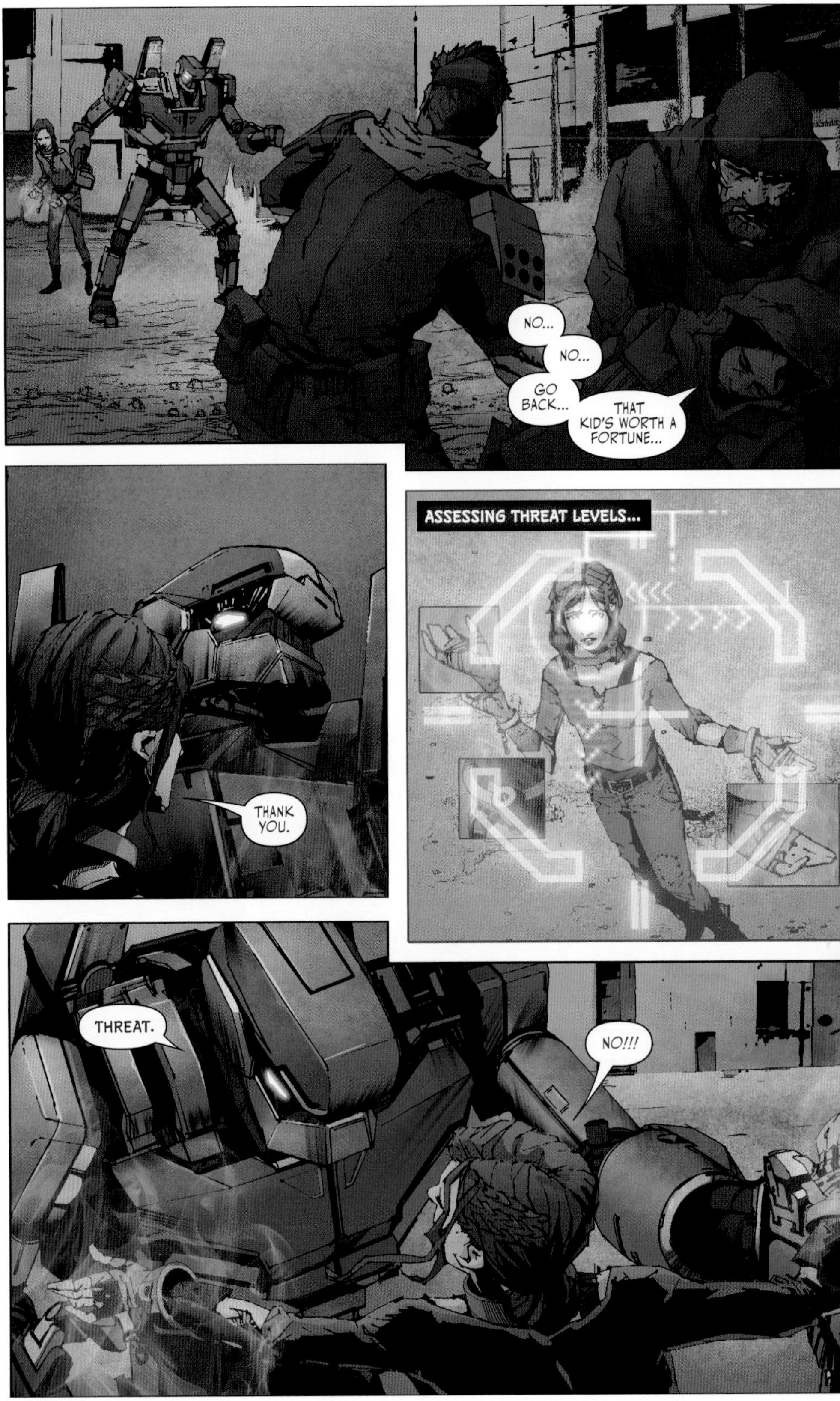
NO...
NO...
GO BACK...
THAT KID'S WORTH A FORTUNE...
THANK YOU.
ASSESSING THREAT LEVELS...
THREAT.
NO!!!

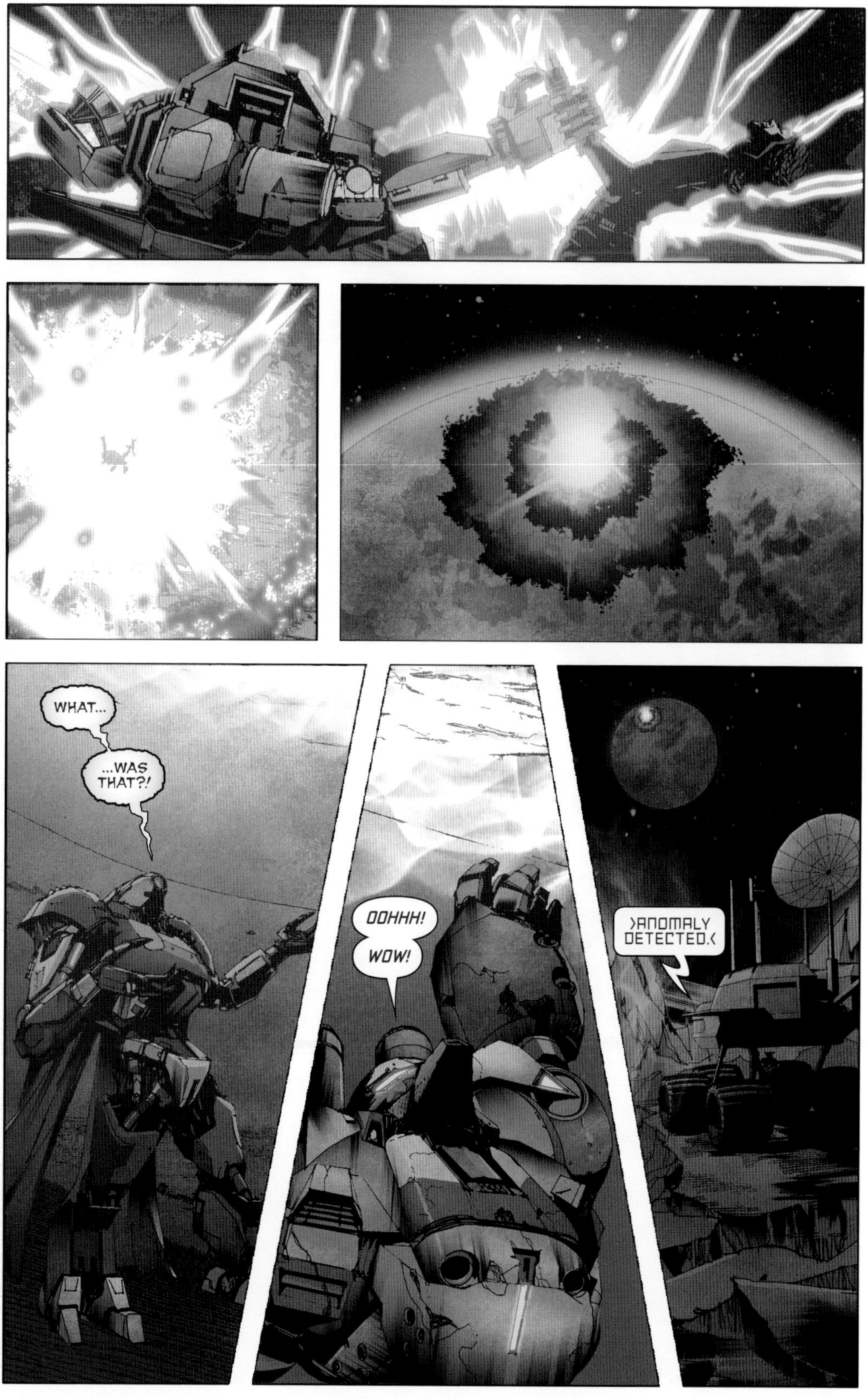
WHAT...
...WAS THAT?!
OOHHH!
WOW!
›ANOMALY DETECTED.‹

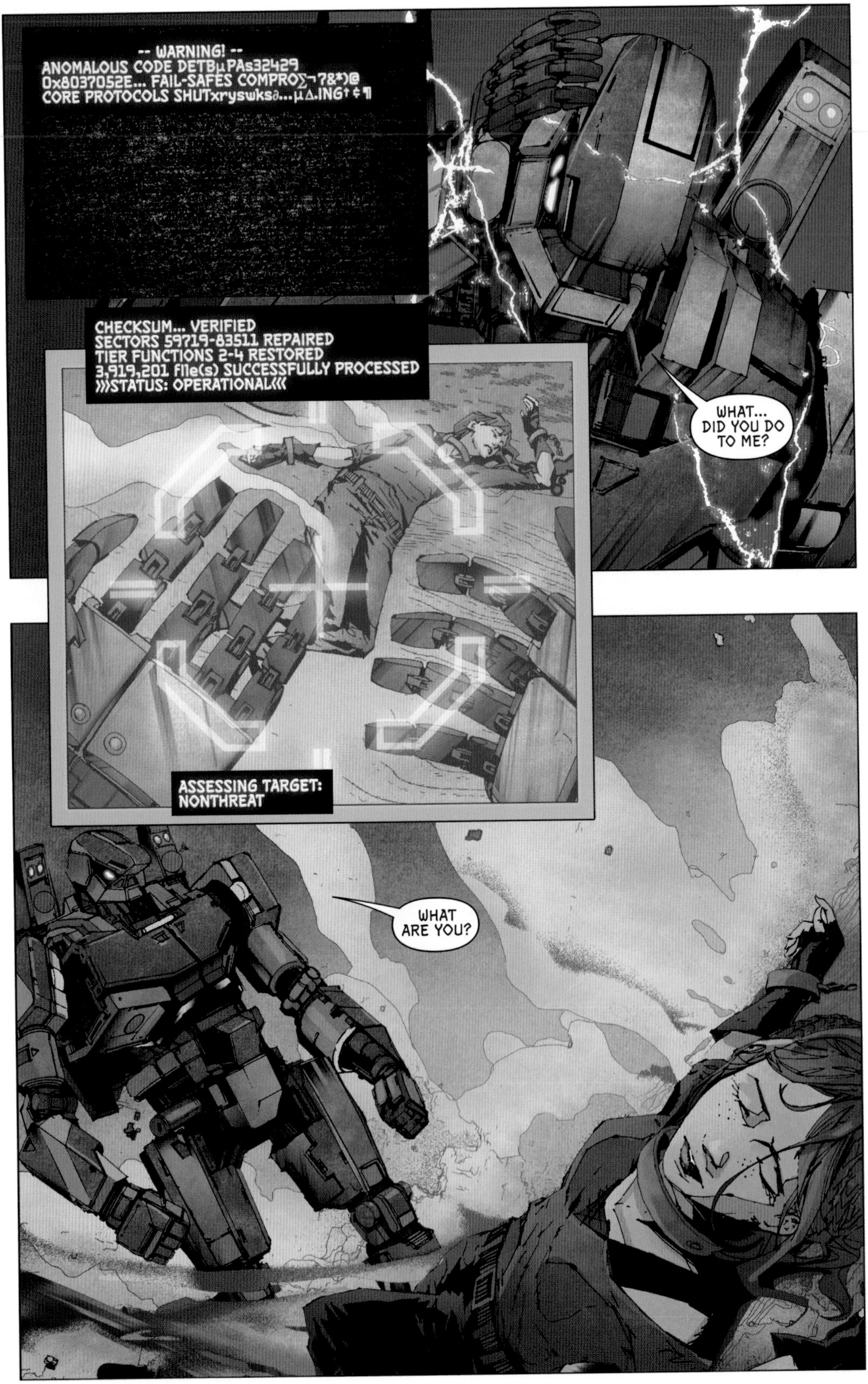
-- WARNING! --
ANOMALOUS CODE DETBµPAs32429
0x8037052E... FAIL-SAFES COMPRO∑¬7&*)@
CORE PROTOCOLS SHUTxryswks∂...µΔ.ING†¢¶
CHECKSUM... VERIFIED
SECTORS 59719-83511 REPAIRED
TIER FUNCTIONS 2-4 RESTORED
3,919,201 file(s) SUCCESSFULLY PROCESSED
»»STATUS: OPERATIONAL««
WHAT... DID YOU DO TO ME?
ASSESSING TARGET: NONTHREAT
WHAT ARE YOU?

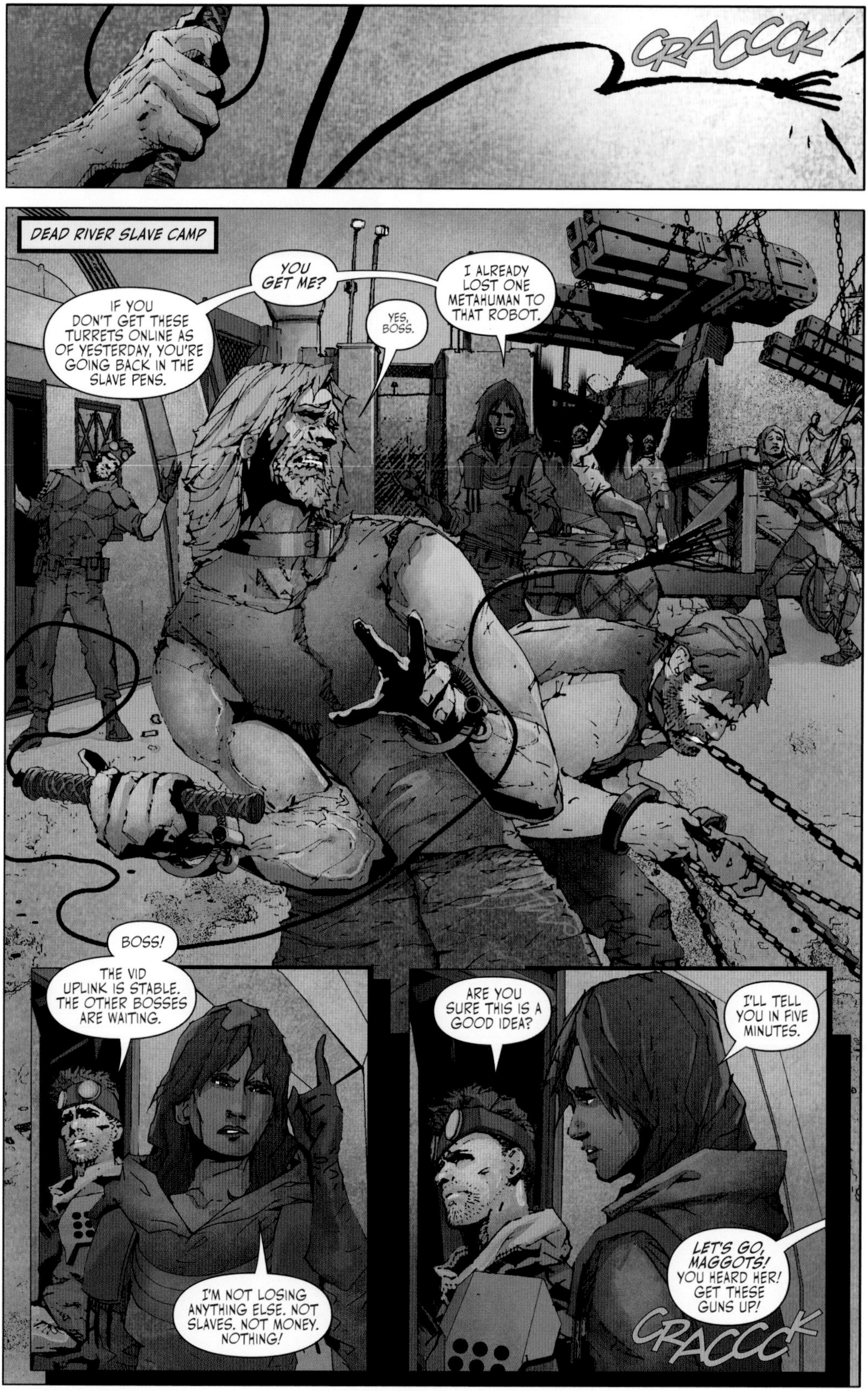
CRACCCK!
DEAD RIVER SLAVE CAMP
IF YOU DON'T GET THESE TURRETS ONLINE AS OF YESTERDAY, YOU'RE GOING BACK IN THE SLAVE PENS.
YOU GET ME?
YES, BOSS.
I ALREADY LOST ONE METAHUMAN TO THAT ROBOT.
BOSS!
THE VID UPLINK IS STABLE. THE OTHER BOSSES ARE WAITING.
I'M NOT LOSING ANYTHING ELSE. NOT SLAVES. NOT MONEY. NOTHING!
ARE YOU SURE THIS IS A GOOD IDEA?
I'LL TELL YOU IN FIVE MINUTES.
LET'S GO, MAGGOTS! YOU HEARD HER! GET THESE GUNS UP!
CRACCCK

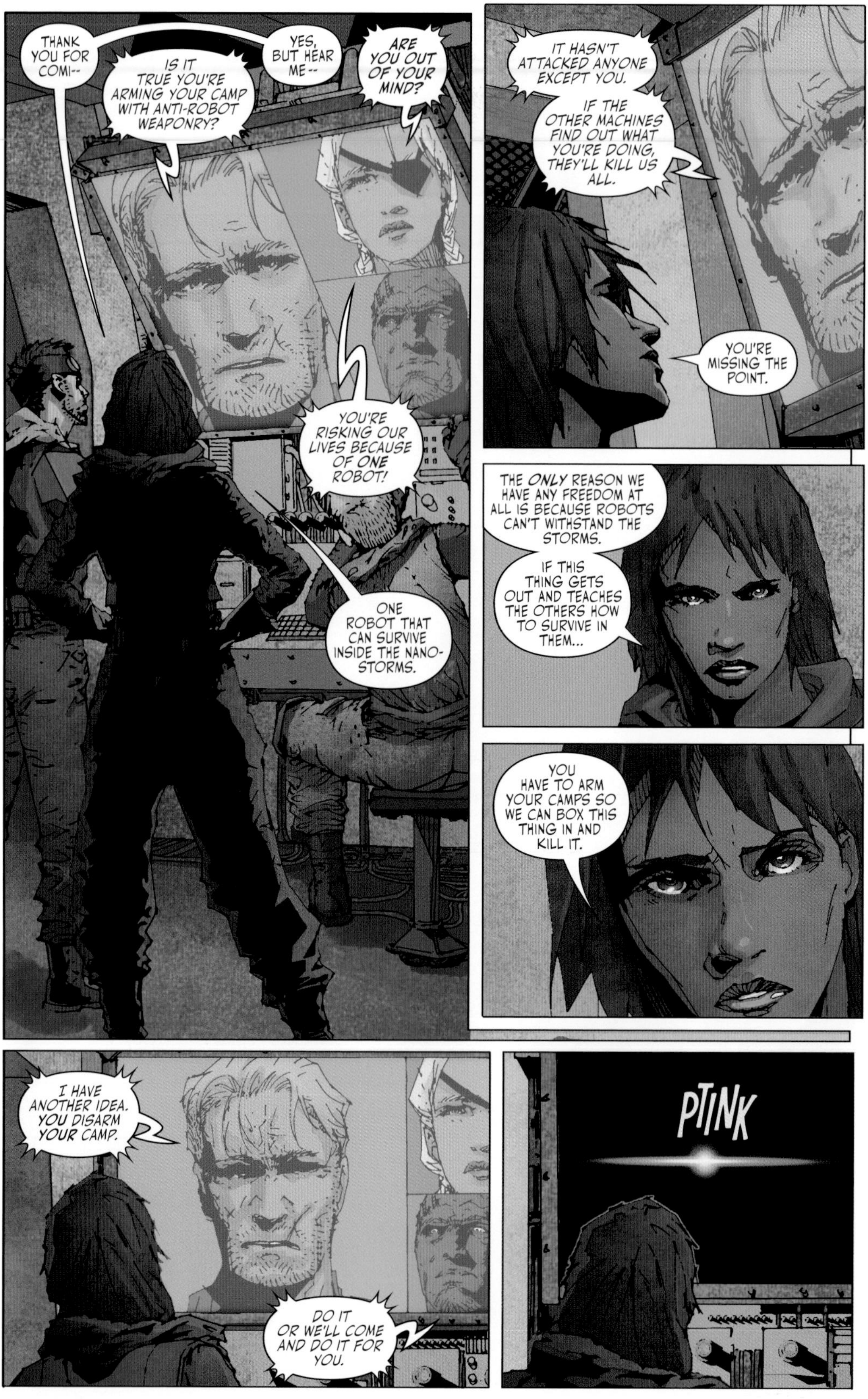
THANK YOU FOR COMI--
IS IT TRUE YOU'RE ARMING YOUR CAMP WITH ANTI-ROBOT WEAPONRY?
YES, BUT HEAR ME--
ARE YOU OUT OF YOUR MIND?
YOU'RE RISKING OUR LIVES BECAUSE OF ONE ROBOT!
ONE ROBOT THAT CAN SURVIVE INSIDE THE NANO-STORMS.
IT HASN'T ATTACKED ANYONE EXCEPT YOU.
IF THE OTHER MACHINES FIND OUT WHAT YOU'RE DOING, THEY'LL KILL US ALL.
YOU'RE MISSING THE POINT.
THE ONLY REASON WE HAVE ANY FREEDOM AT ALL IS BECAUSE ROBOTS CAN'T WITHSTAND THE STORMS.
IF THIS THING GETS OUT AND TEACHES THE OTHERS HOW TO SURVIVE IN THEM...
YOU HAVE TO ARM YOUR CAMPS SO WE CAN BOX THIS THING IN AND KILL IT.
I HAVE ANOTHER IDEA. YOU DISARM YOUR CAMP.
DO IT OR WE'LL COME AND DO IT FOR YOU.
PTINK

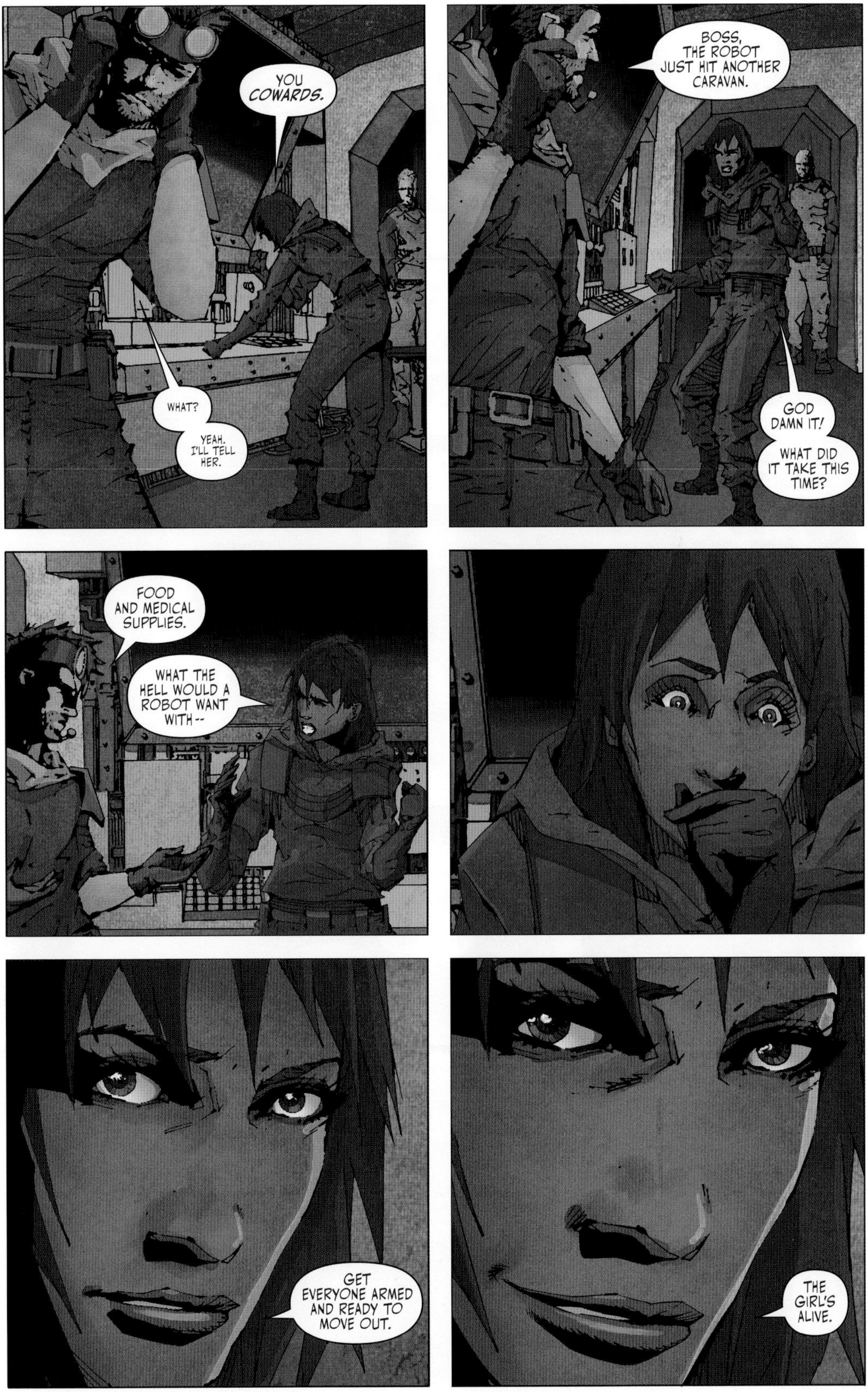
YOU COWARDS.
WHAT?
YEAH. I'LL TELL HER.
BOSS, THE ROBOT JUST HIT ANOTHER CARAVAN.
GOD DAMN IT!
WHAT DID IT TAKE THIS TIME?
FOOD AND MEDICAL SUPPLIES.
WHAT THE HELL WOULD A ROBOT WANT WITH --
GET EVERYONE ARMED AND READY TO MOVE OUT.
THE GIRL'S ALIVE.

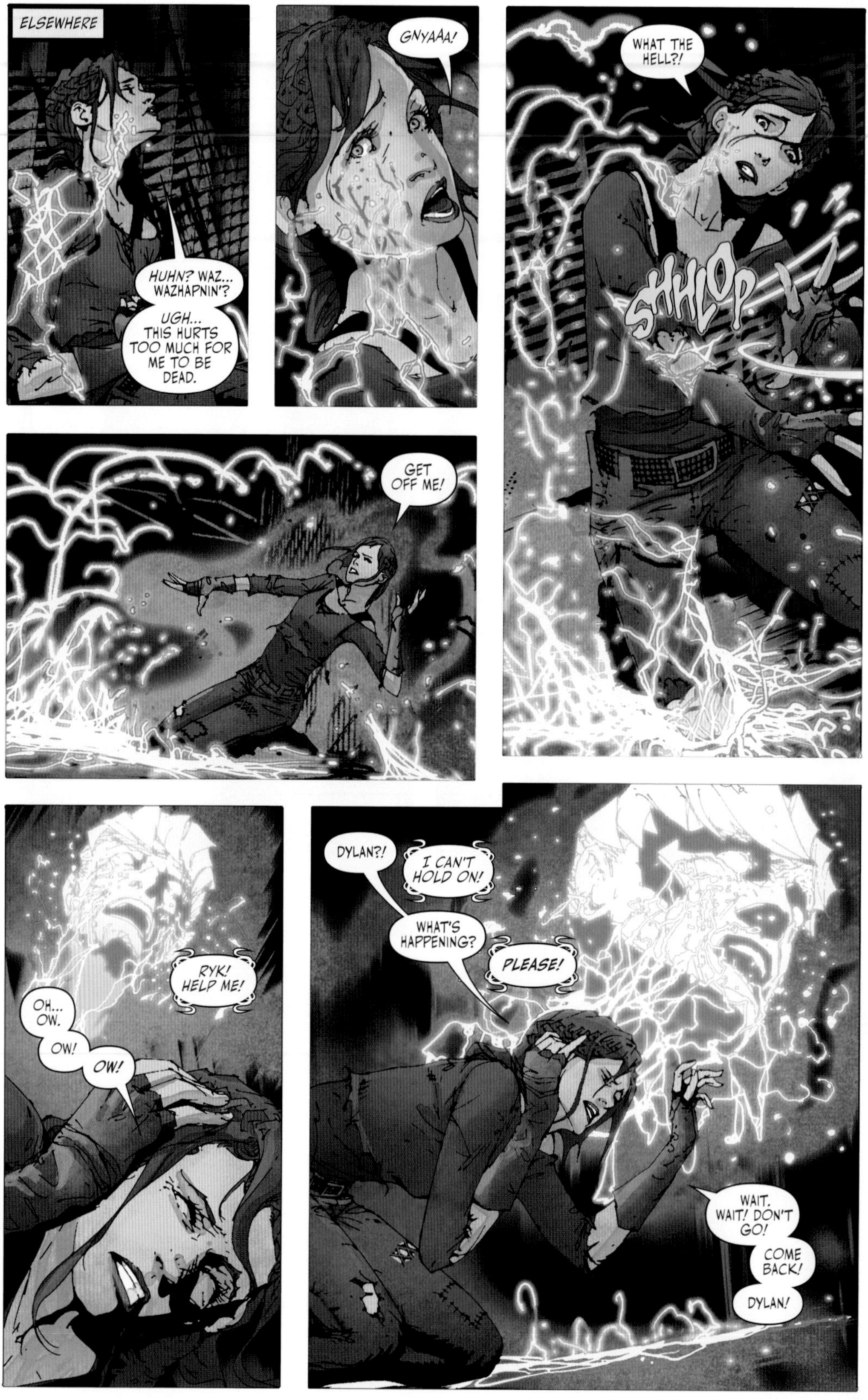
ELSEWHERE
HUHN? WAZ... WAZHAPNIN'?
UGH... THIS HURTS TOO MUCH FOR ME TO BE DEAD.
GNYAAA!
WHAT THE HELL?!
SHHLOP
GET OFF ME!
RYK! HELP ME!
OH... OW.
OW!
OW!
DYLAN?!
I CAN'T HOLD ON!
WHAT'S HAPPENING?
PLEASE!
WAIT. WAIT! DON'T GO!
COME BACK!
DYLAN!

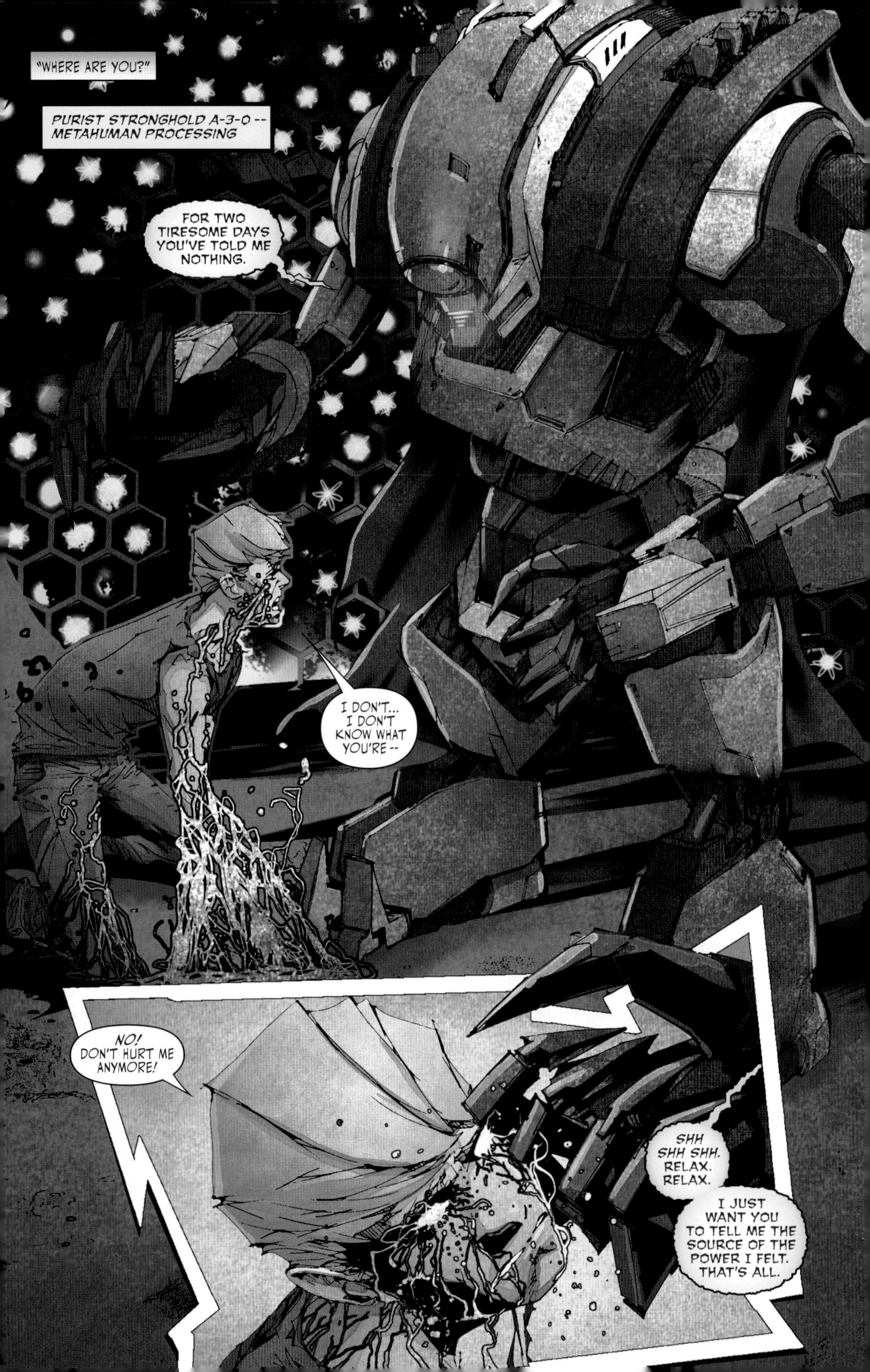
"WHERE ARE YOU?"
PURIST STRONGHOLD A-3-0 -- METAHUMAN PROCESSING
FOR TWO TIRESOME DAYS YOU'VE TOLD ME NOTHING.
I DON'T... I DON'T KNOW WHAT YOU'RE --
NO! DON'T HURT ME ANYMORE!
SHH SHH SHH. RELAX. RELAX.
I JUST WANT YOU TO TELL ME THE SOURCE OF THE POWER I FELT. THAT'S ALL.

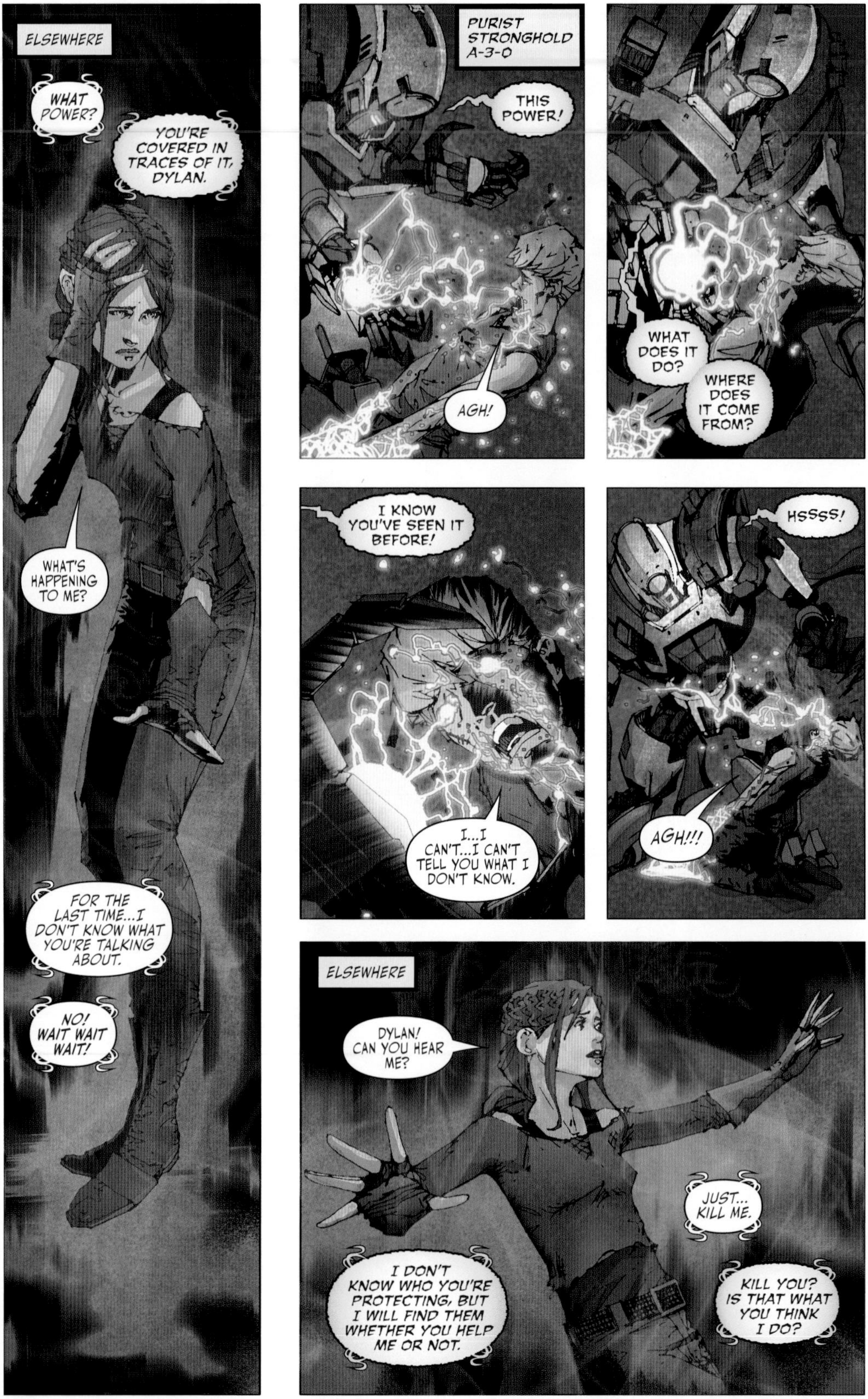
ELSEWHERE
WHAT POWER?
YOU'RE COVERED IN TRACES OF IT, DYLAN.
WHAT'S HAPPENING TO ME?
FOR THE LAST TIME...I DON'T KNOW WHAT YOU'RE TALKING ABOUT.
NO! WAIT WAIT WAIT!
PURIST STRONGHOLD A-3-0
THIS POWER!
AGH!
WHAT DOES IT DO?
WHERE DOES IT COME FROM?
I KNOW YOU'VE SEEN IT BEFORE!
I...I CAN'T...I CAN'T TELL YOU WHAT I DON'T KNOW.
HSSSS!
AGH!!!
ELSEWHERE
DYLAN! CAN YOU HEAR ME?
JUST... KILL ME.
I DON'T KNOW WHO YOU'RE PROTECTING, BUT I WILL FIND THEM WHETHER YOU HELP ME OR NOT.
KILL YOU? IS THAT WHAT YOU THINK I DO?

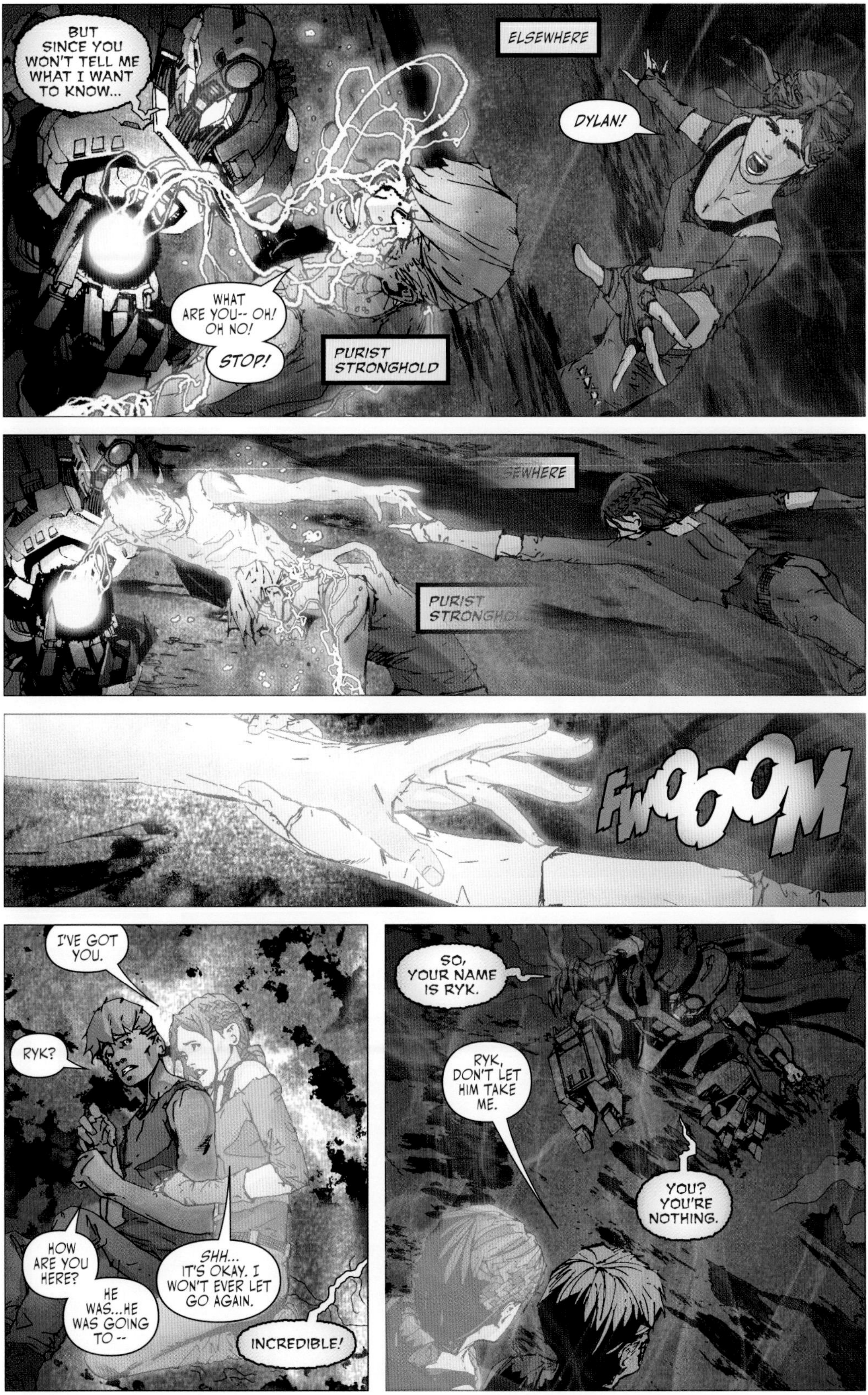
BUT SINCE YOU WON'T TELL ME WHAT I WANT TO KNOW...
ELSEWHERE
DYLAN!
WHAT ARE YOU-- OH! OH NO!
STOP!
PURIST STRONGHOLD
SEWHERE
PURIST STRONGHO
FWOOOM
I'VE GOT YOU.
RYK?
HOW ARE YOU HERE?
HE WAS...HE WAS GOING TO --
SHH... IT'S OKAY. I WON'T EVER LET GO AGAIN.
INCREDIBLE!
SO, YOUR NAME IS RYK.
RYK, DON'T LET HIM TAKE ME.
YOU? YOU'RE NOTHING.

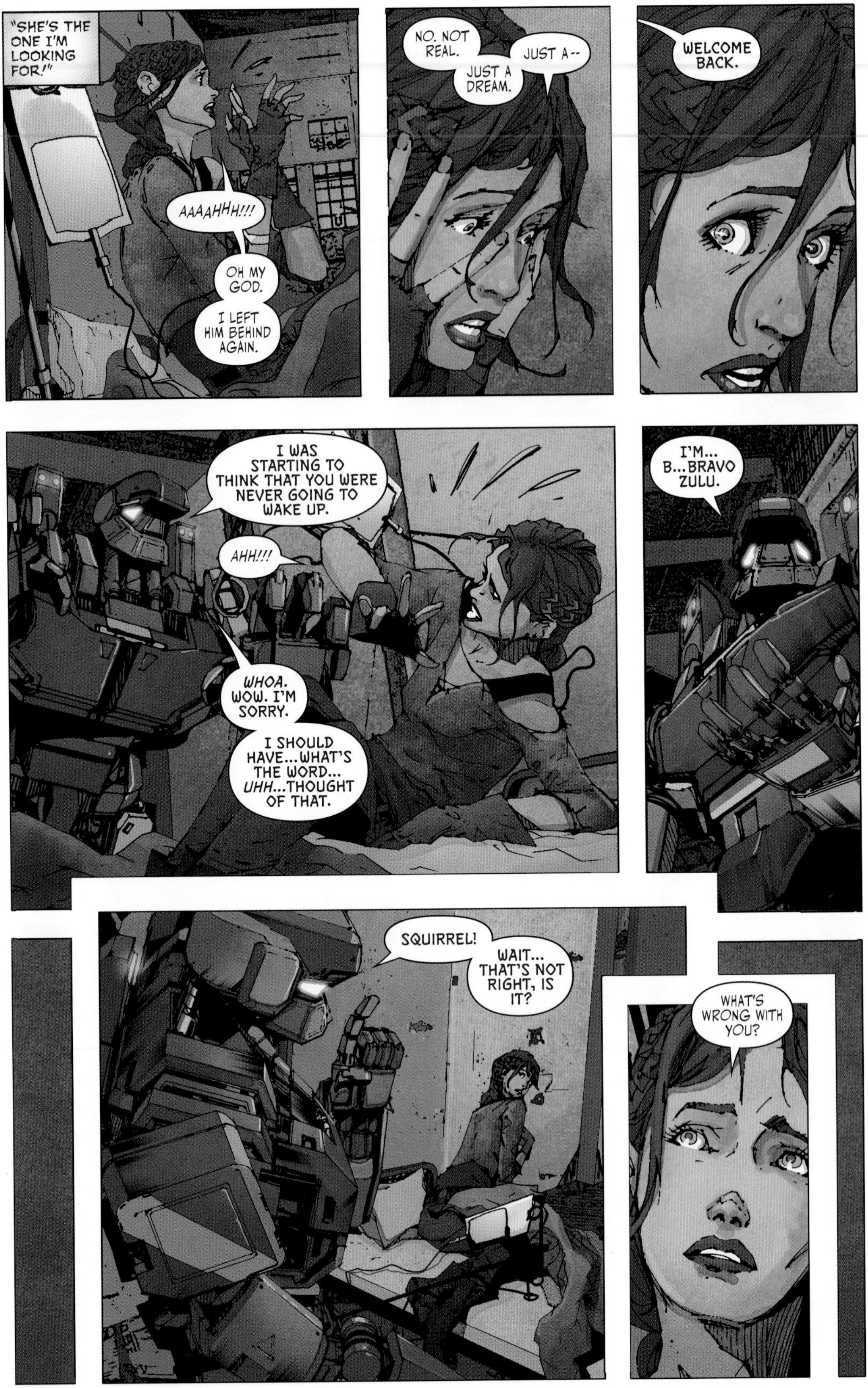
"SHE'S THE ONE I'M LOOKING FOR!"
AAAAHHH!!!
OH MY GOD.
I LEFT HIM BEHIND AGAIN.
NO. NOT REAL.
JUST A DREAM.
JUST A--
WELCOME BACK.
I WAS STARTING TO THINK THAT YOU WERE NEVER GOING TO WAKE UP.
AHH!!!
WHOA. WOW. I'M SORRY.
I SHOULD HAVE...WHAT'S THE WORD... UHH...THOUGHT OF THAT.
I'M... B...BRAVO ZULU.
SQUIRREL!
WAIT... THAT'S NOT RIGHT, IS IT?
WHAT'S WRONG WITH YOU?

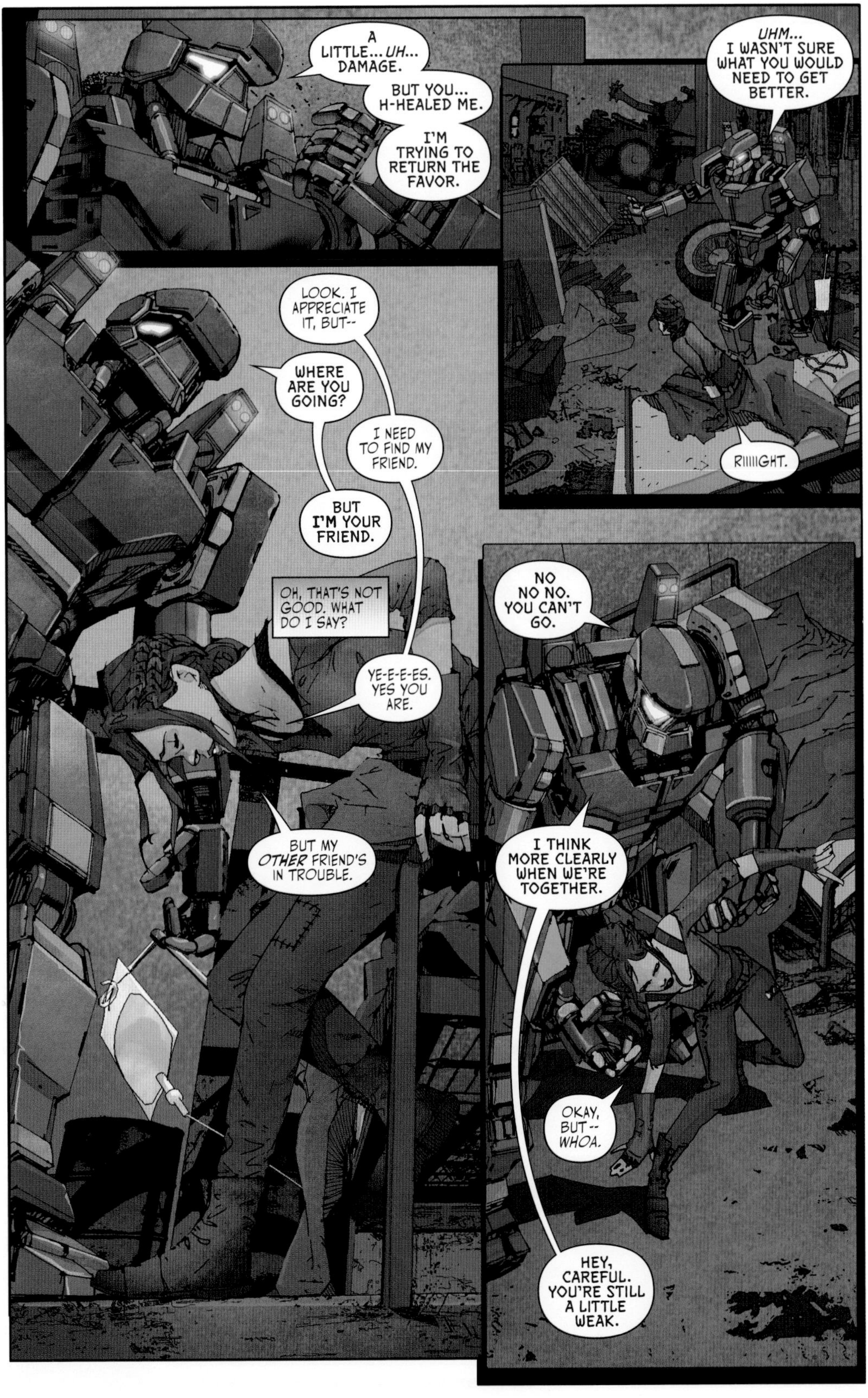
A LITTLE... UH... DAMAGE.
BUT YOU... H-HEALED ME.
I'M TRYING TO RETURN THE FAVOR.
UHM... I WASN'T SURE WHAT YOU WOULD NEED TO GET BETTER.
RIIIIGHT.
LOOK. I APPRECIATE IT, BUT--
WHERE ARE YOU GOING?
I NEED TO FIND MY FRIEND.
BUT I'M YOUR FRIEND.
OH, THAT'S NOT GOOD. WHAT DO I SAY?
YE-E-E-ES. YES YOU ARE.
BUT MY OTHER FRIEND'S IN TROUBLE.
NO NO NO. YOU CAN'T GO.
I THINK MORE CLEARLY WHEN WE'RE TOGETHER.
OKAY, BUT-- WHOA.
HEY, CAREFUL. YOU'RE STILL A LITTLE WEAK.

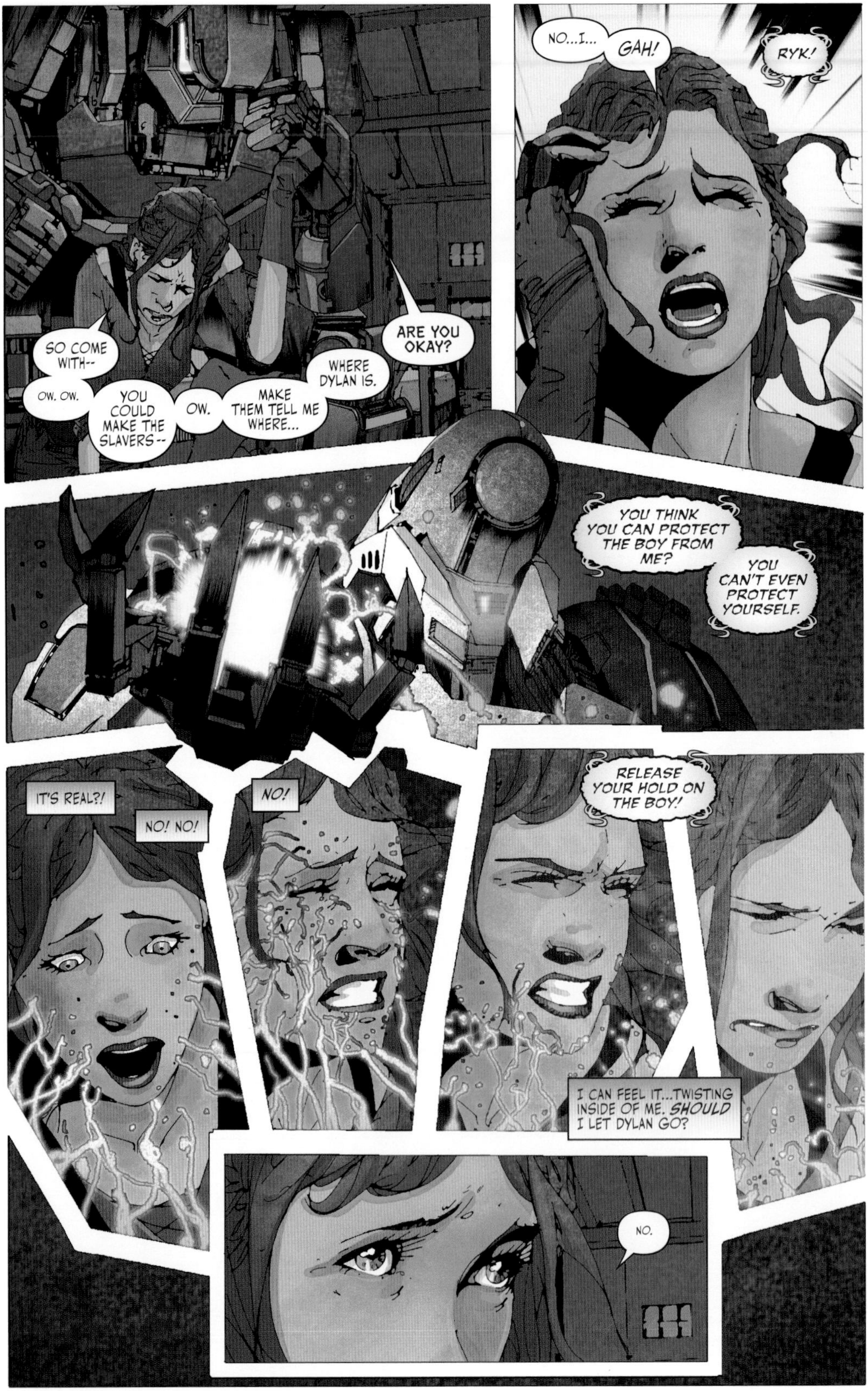
SO COME WITH--
OW. OW.
YOU COULD MAKE THE SLAVERS--
OW.
MAKE THEM TELL ME WHERE...
WHERE DYLAN IS.
ARE YOU OKAY?
NO...I...
GAH!
RYK!
YOU THINK YOU CAN PROTECT THE BOY FROM ME?
YOU CAN'T EVEN PROTECT YOURSELF.
IT'S REAL?!
NO! NO!
NO!
RELEASE YOUR HOLD ON THE BOY!
I CAN FEEL IT...TWISTING INSIDE OF ME. SHOULD I LET DYLAN GO?
NO.

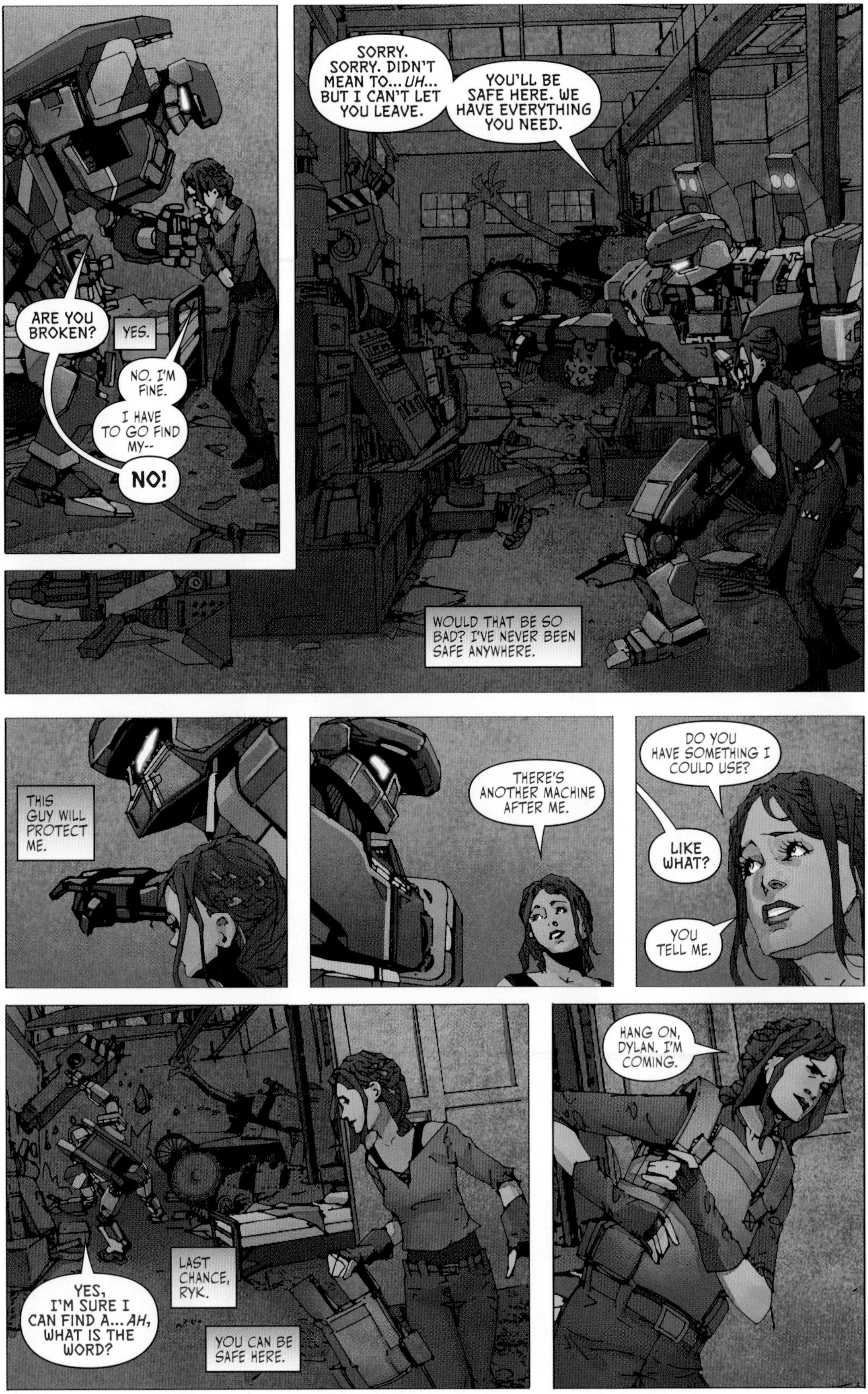
ARE YOU BROKEN?
YES.
NO. I'M FINE.
I HAVE TO GO FIND MY--
NO!
SORRY. SORRY. DIDN'T MEAN TO... *UH*... BUT I CAN'T LET YOU LEAVE.
YOU'LL BE SAFE HERE. WE HAVE EVERYTHING YOU NEED.
WOULD THAT BE SO BAD? I'VE NEVER BEEN SAFE ANYWHERE.
THIS GUY WILL PROTECT ME.
THERE'S ANOTHER MACHINE AFTER ME.
DO YOU HAVE SOMETHING I COULD USE?
LIKE WHAT?
YOU TELL ME.
YES, I'M SURE I CAN FIND A... *AH*, WHAT IS THE WORD?
LAST CHANCE, RYK.
YOU CAN BE SAFE HERE.
HANG ON, DYLAN. I'M COMING.

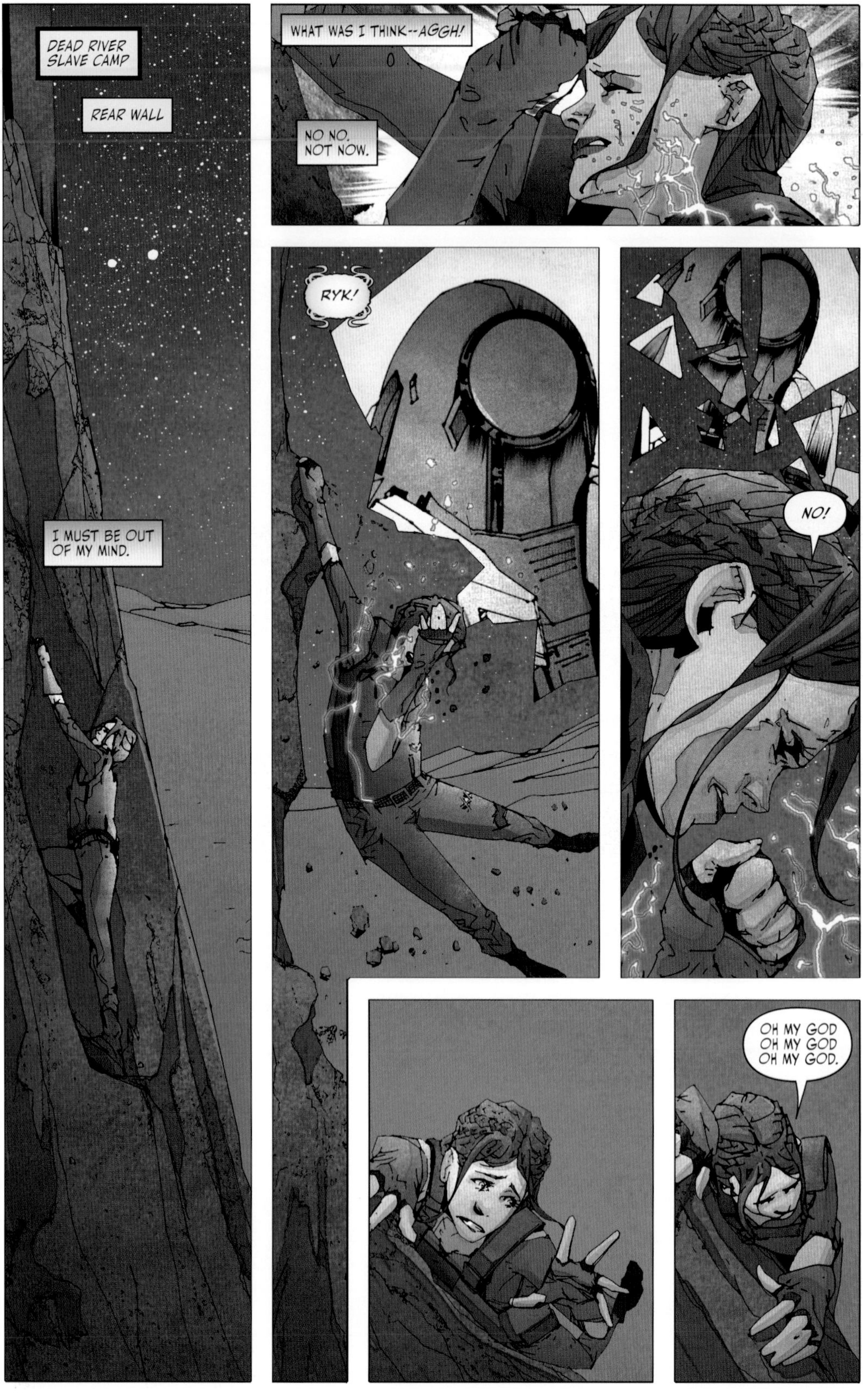
DEAD RIVER SLAVE CAMP
REAR WALL
I MUST BE OUT OF MY MIND.
WHAT WAS I THINK--AGGH!
NO NO. NOT NOW.
RYK!
NO!
OH MY GOD OH MY GOD OH MY GOD.

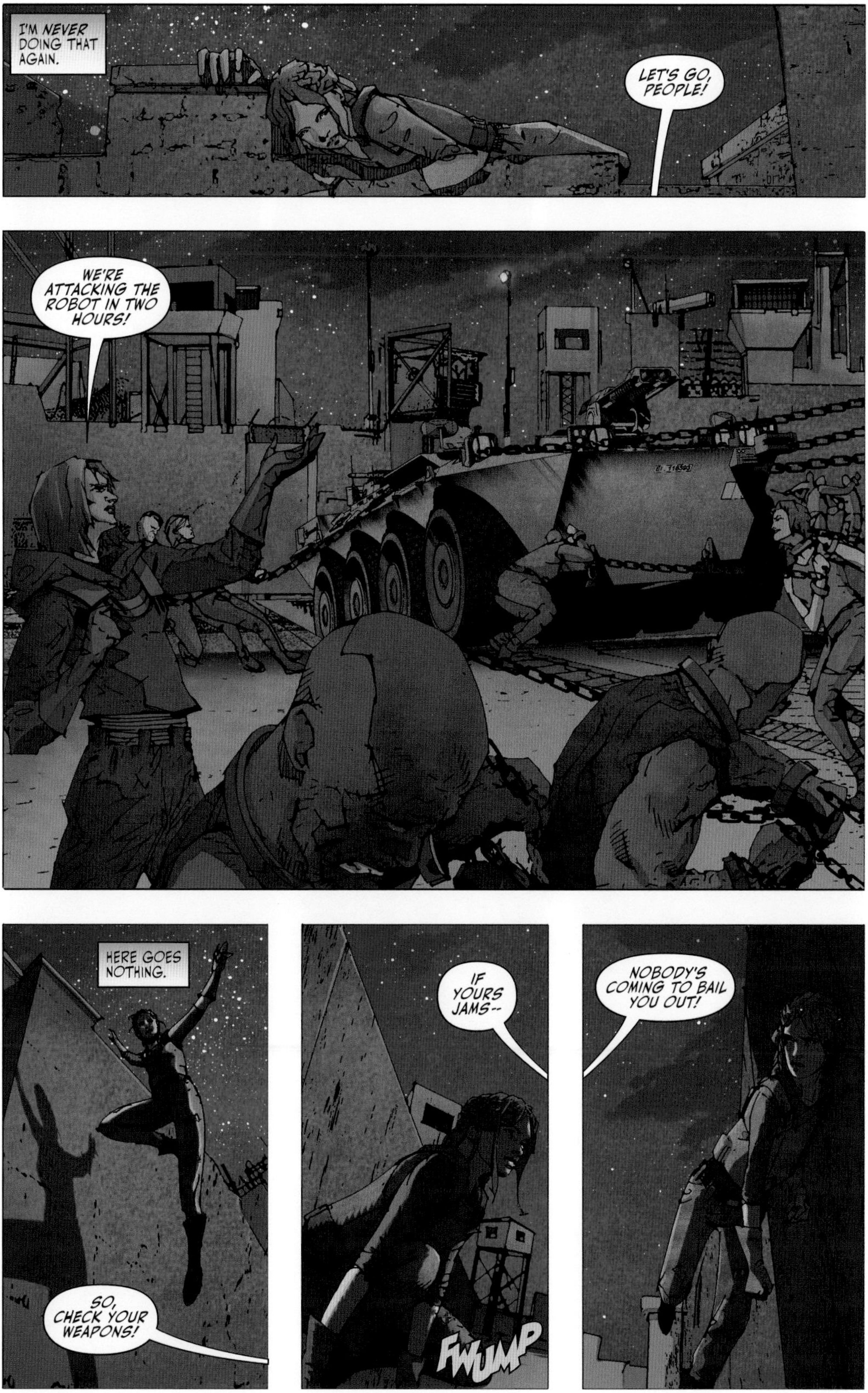
I'M NEVER DOING THAT AGAIN.
LET'S GO, PEOPLE!
WE'RE ATTACKING THE ROBOT IN TWO HOURS!
HERE GOES NOTHING.
SO, CHECK YOUR WEAPONS!
IF YOURS JAMS--
FWUMP
NOBODY'S COMING TO BAIL YOU OUT!

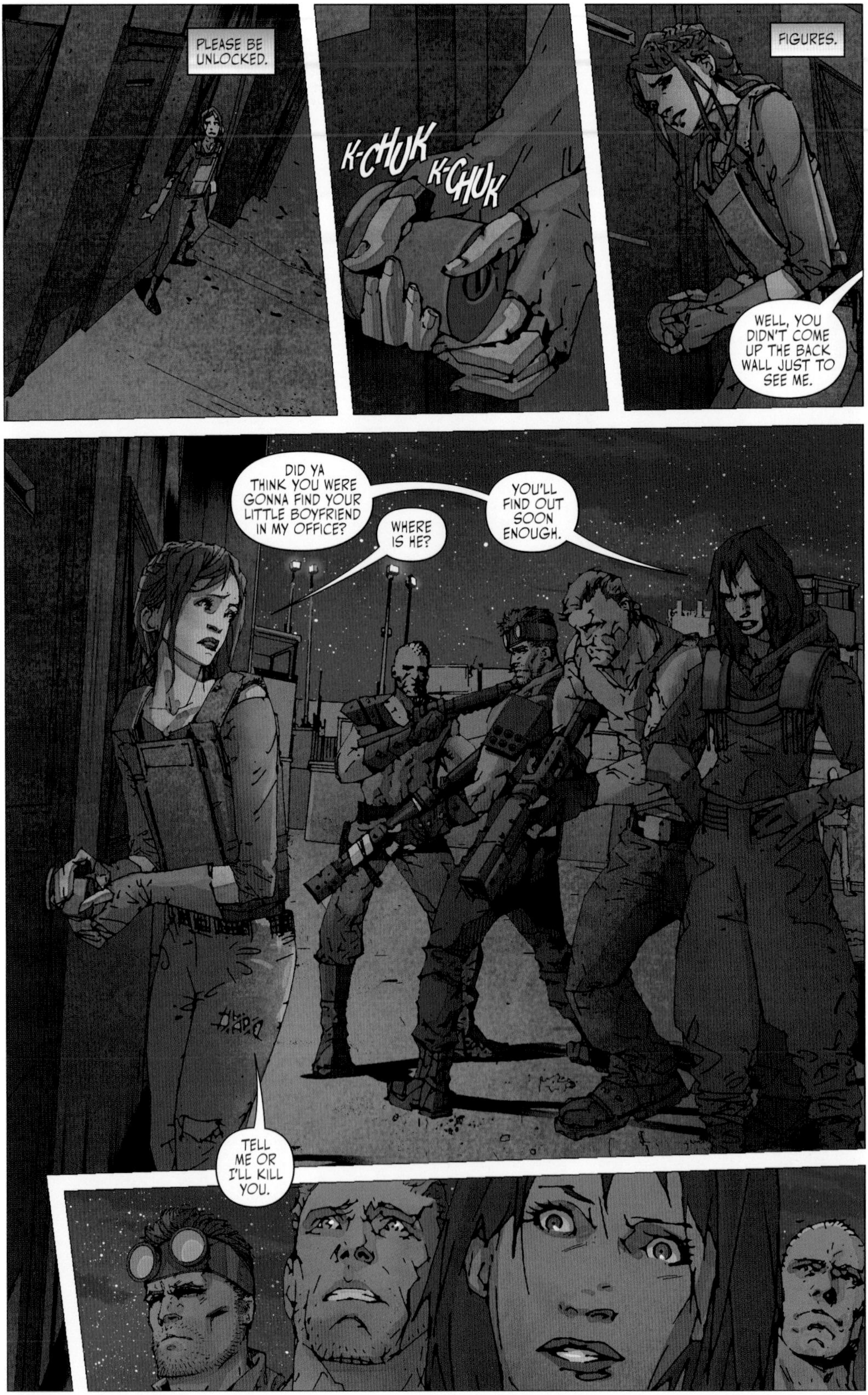

PLEASE BE UNLOCKED.
K-CHUK K-CHUK
FIGURES.
WELL, YOU DIDN'T COME UP THE BACK WALL JUST TO SEE ME.
DID YA THINK YOU WERE GONNA FIND YOUR LITTLE BOYFRIEND IN MY OFFICE?
WHERE IS HE?
YOU'LL FIND OUT SOON ENOUGH.
TELL ME OR I'LL KILL YOU.

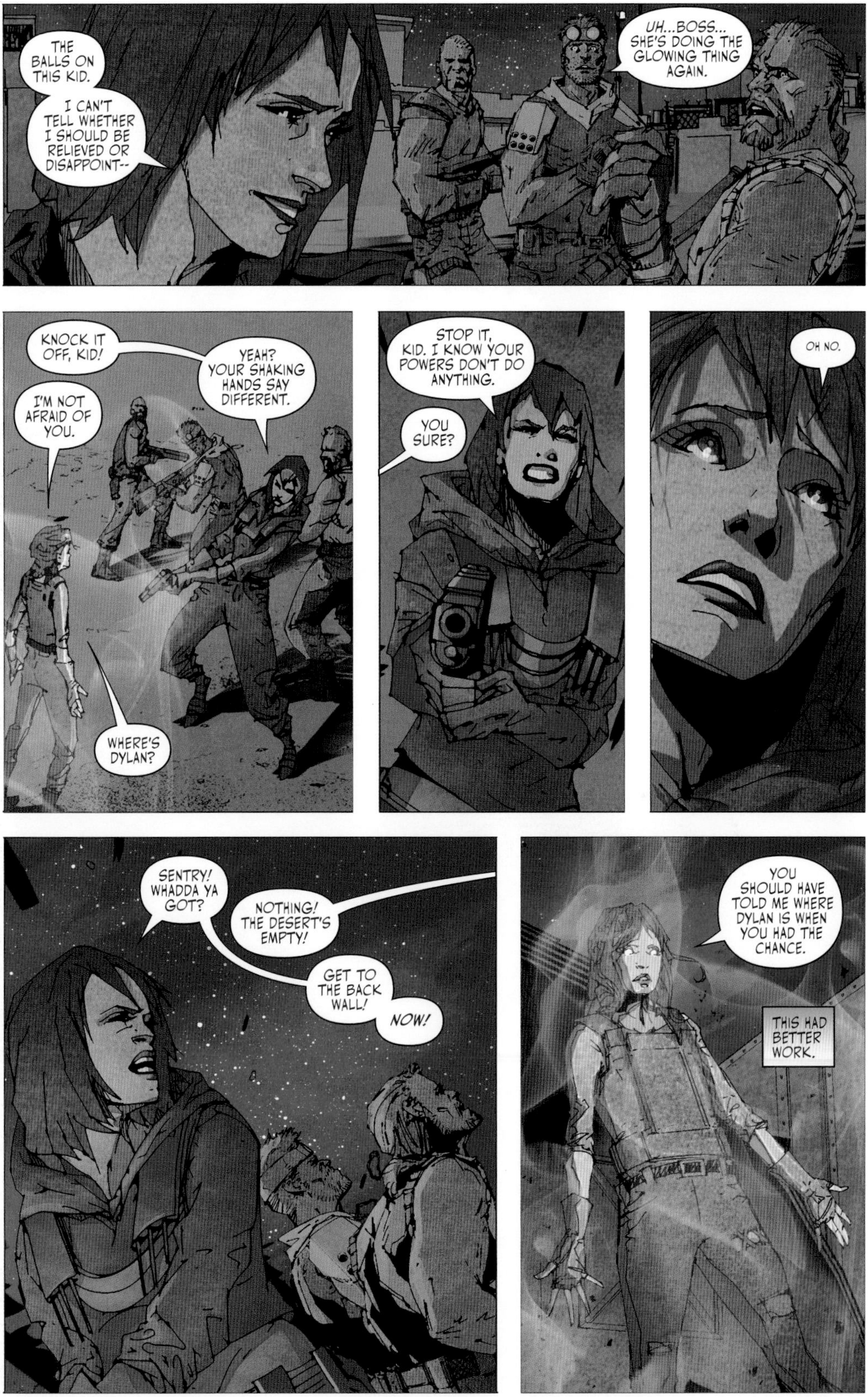
THE BALLS ON THIS KID.
I CAN'T TELL WHETHER I SHOULD BE RELIEVED OR DISAPPOINT--
UH...BOSS... SHE'S DOING THE GLOWING THING AGAIN.
KNOCK IT OFF, KID!
I'M NOT AFRAID OF YOU.
YEAH? YOUR SHAKING HANDS SAY DIFFERENT.
WHERE'S DYLAN?
STOP IT, KID. I KNOW YOUR POWERS DON'T DO ANYTHING.
YOU SURE?
OH NO.
SENTRY! WHADDA YA GOT?
NOTHING! THE DESERT'S EMPTY!
GET TO THE BACK WALL!
NOW!
YOU SHOULD HAVE TOLD ME WHERE DYLAN IS WHEN YOU HAD THE CHANCE.
THIS HAD BETTER WORK.

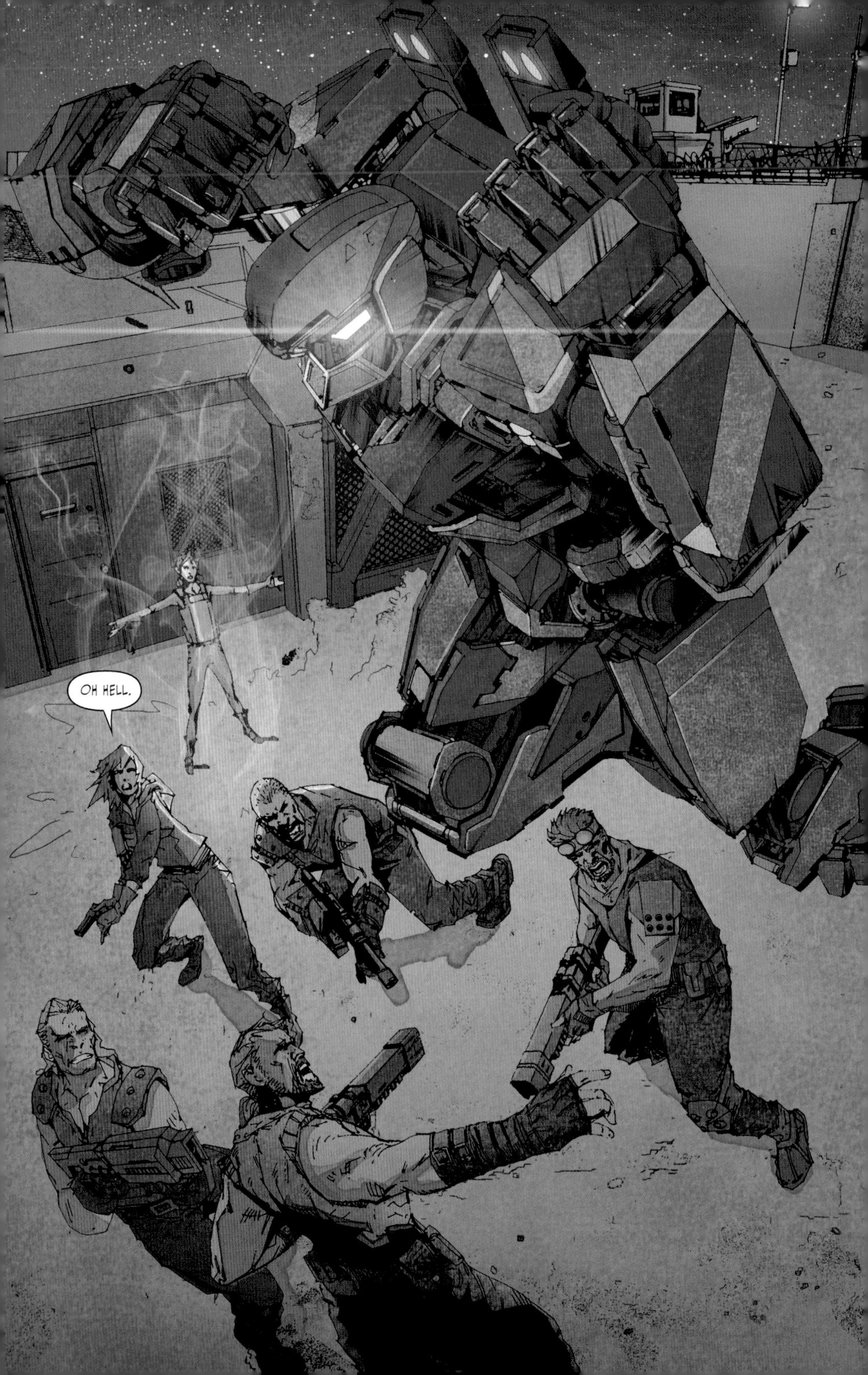
OH HELL.

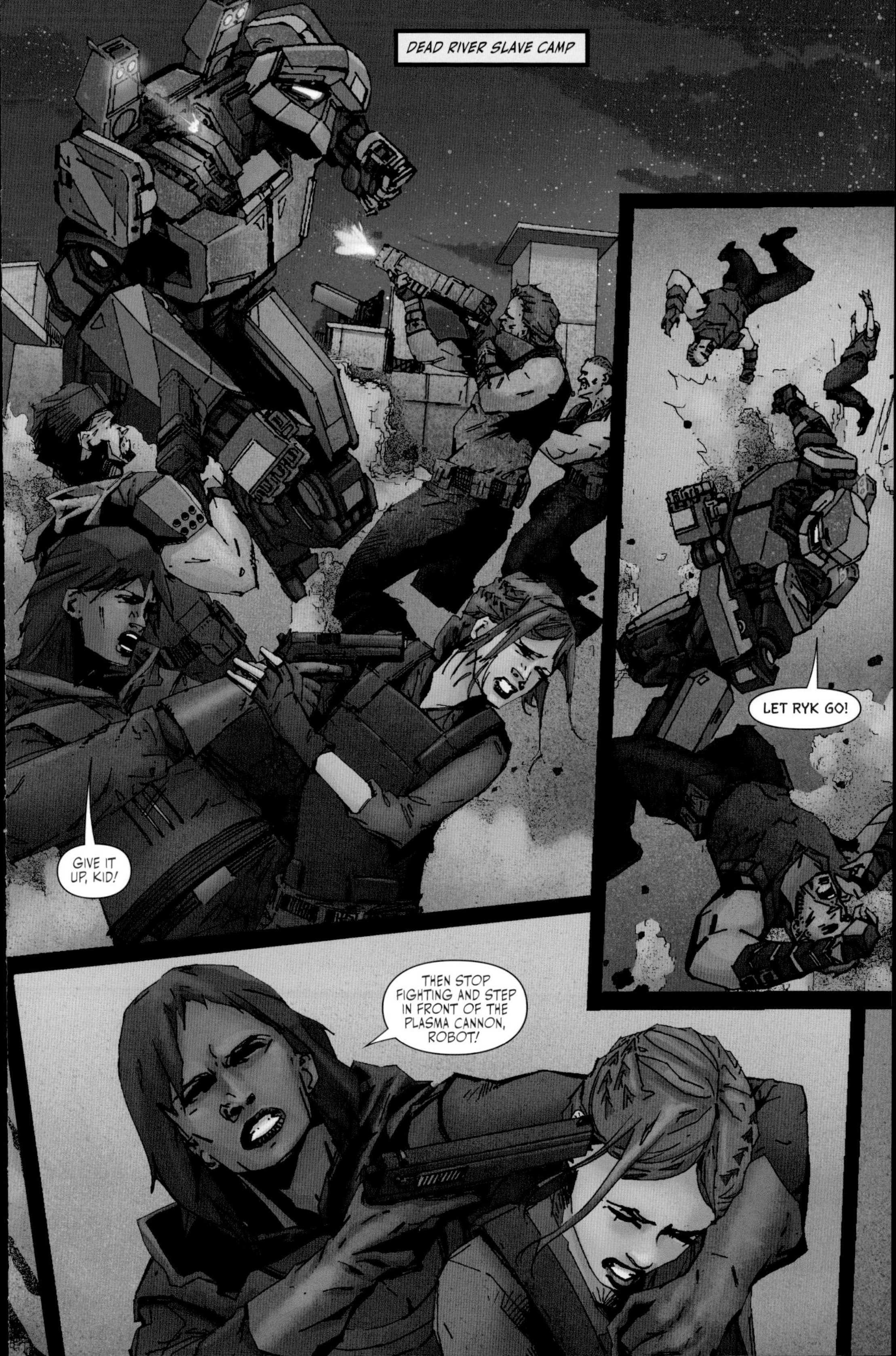
DEAD RIVER SLAVE CAMP
GIVE IT UP, KID!
LET RYK GO!
THEN STOP FIGHTING AND STEP IN FRONT OF THE PLASMA CANNON, ROBOT!

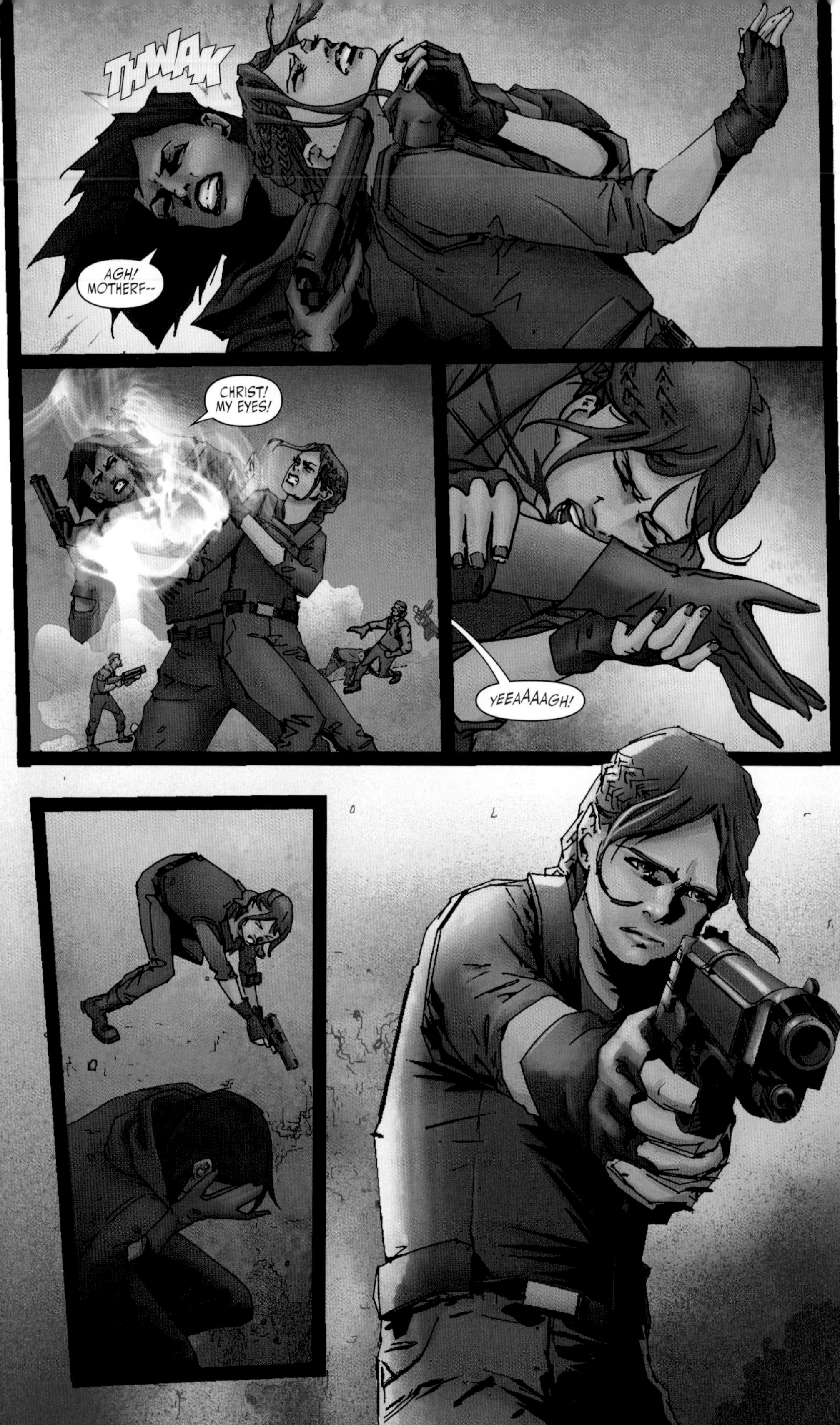
THWAK
AGH! MOTHERF--
CHRIST! MY EYES!
YEEAAAAGH!

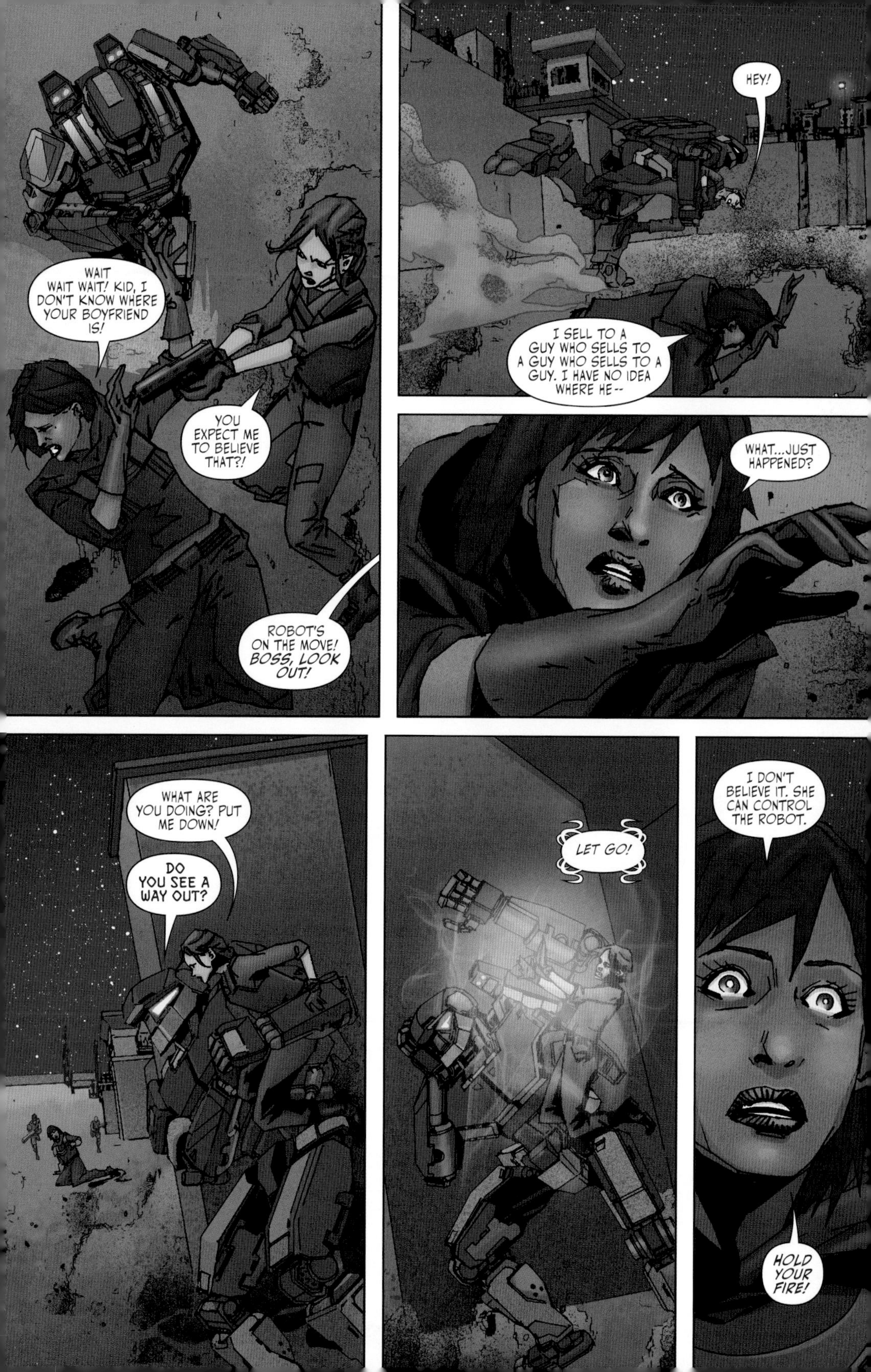
WAIT WAIT WAIT! KID, I DON'T KNOW WHERE YOUR BOYFRIEND IS!
YOU EXPECT ME TO BELIEVE THAT?!
ROBOT'S ON THE MOVE! BOSS, LOOK OUT!
HEY!
I SELL TO A GUY WHO SELLS TO A GUY WHO SELLS TO A GUY. I HAVE NO IDEA WHERE HE--
WHAT...JUST HAPPENED?
WHAT ARE YOU DOING? PUT ME DOWN!
DO YOU SEE A WAY OUT?
LET GO!
I DON'T BELIEVE IT. SHE CAN CONTROL THE ROBOT.
HOLD YOUR FIRE!

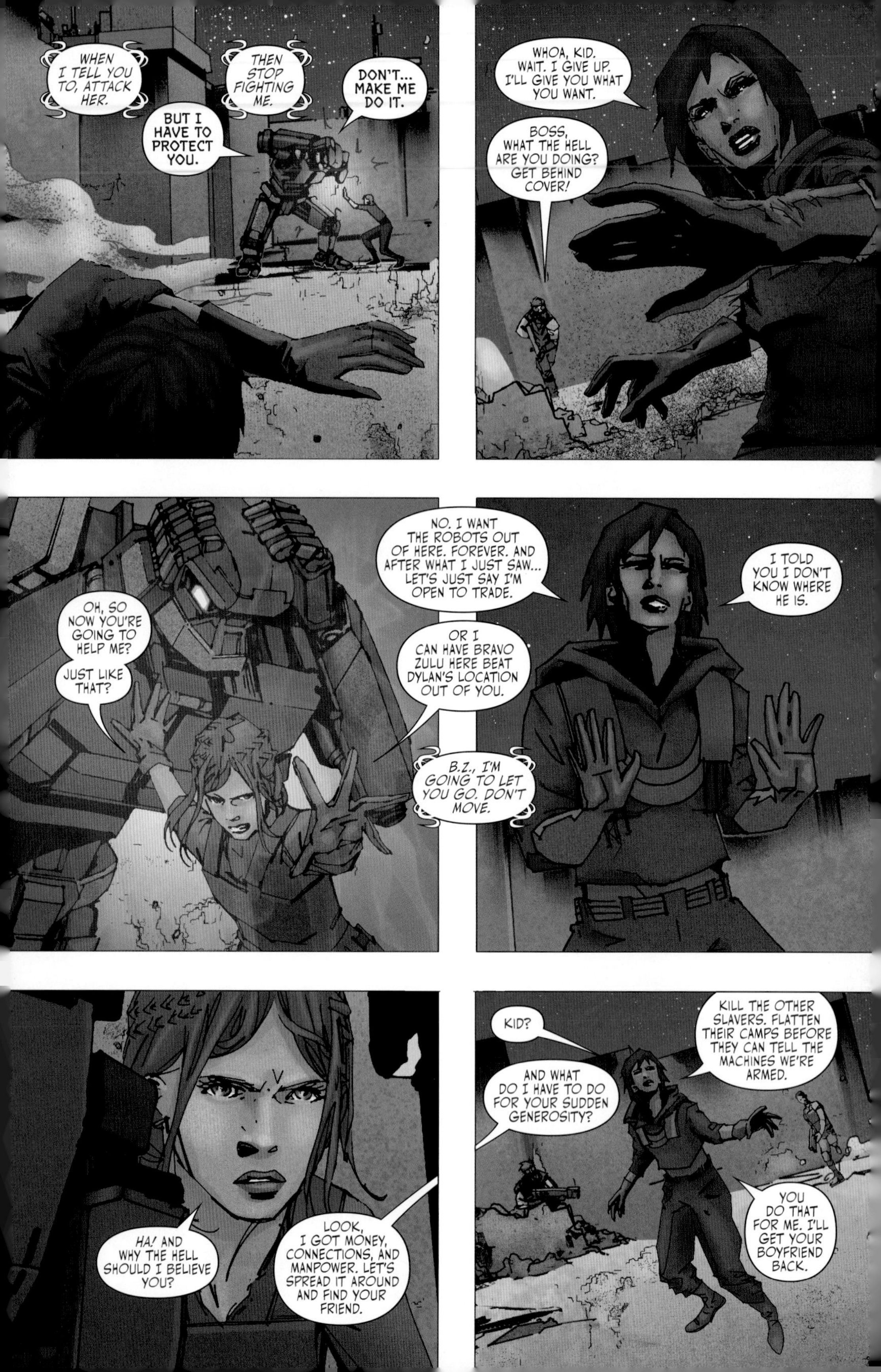

WHEN I TELL YOU TO, ATTACK HER.
BUT I HAVE TO PROTECT YOU.
THEN STOP FIGHTING ME.
DON'T... MAKE ME DO IT.
WHOA, KID. WAIT. I GIVE UP. I'LL GIVE YOU WHAT YOU WANT.
BOSS, WHAT THE HELL ARE YOU DOING? GET BEHIND COVER!
OH, SO NOW YOU'RE GOING TO HELP ME?
JUST LIKE THAT?
NO. I WANT THE ROBOTS OUT OF HERE. FOREVER. AND AFTER WHAT I JUST SAW... LET'S JUST SAY I'M OPEN TO TRADE.
OR I CAN HAVE BRAVO ZULU HERE BEAT DYLAN'S LOCATION OUT OF YOU.
B.Z., I'M GOING TO LET YOU GO. DON'T MOVE.
I TOLD YOU I DON'T KNOW WHERE HE IS.
HA! AND WHY THE HELL SHOULD I BELIEVE YOU?
LOOK, I GOT MONEY, CONNECTIONS, AND MANPOWER. LET'S SPREAD IT AROUND AND FIND YOUR FRIEND.
KID?
AND WHAT DO I HAVE TO DO FOR YOUR SUDDEN GENEROSITY?
KILL THE OTHER SLAVERS. FLATTEN THEIR CAMPS BEFORE THEY CAN TELL THE MACHINES WE'RE ARMED.
YOU DO THAT FOR ME. I'LL GET YOUR BOYFRIEND BACK.

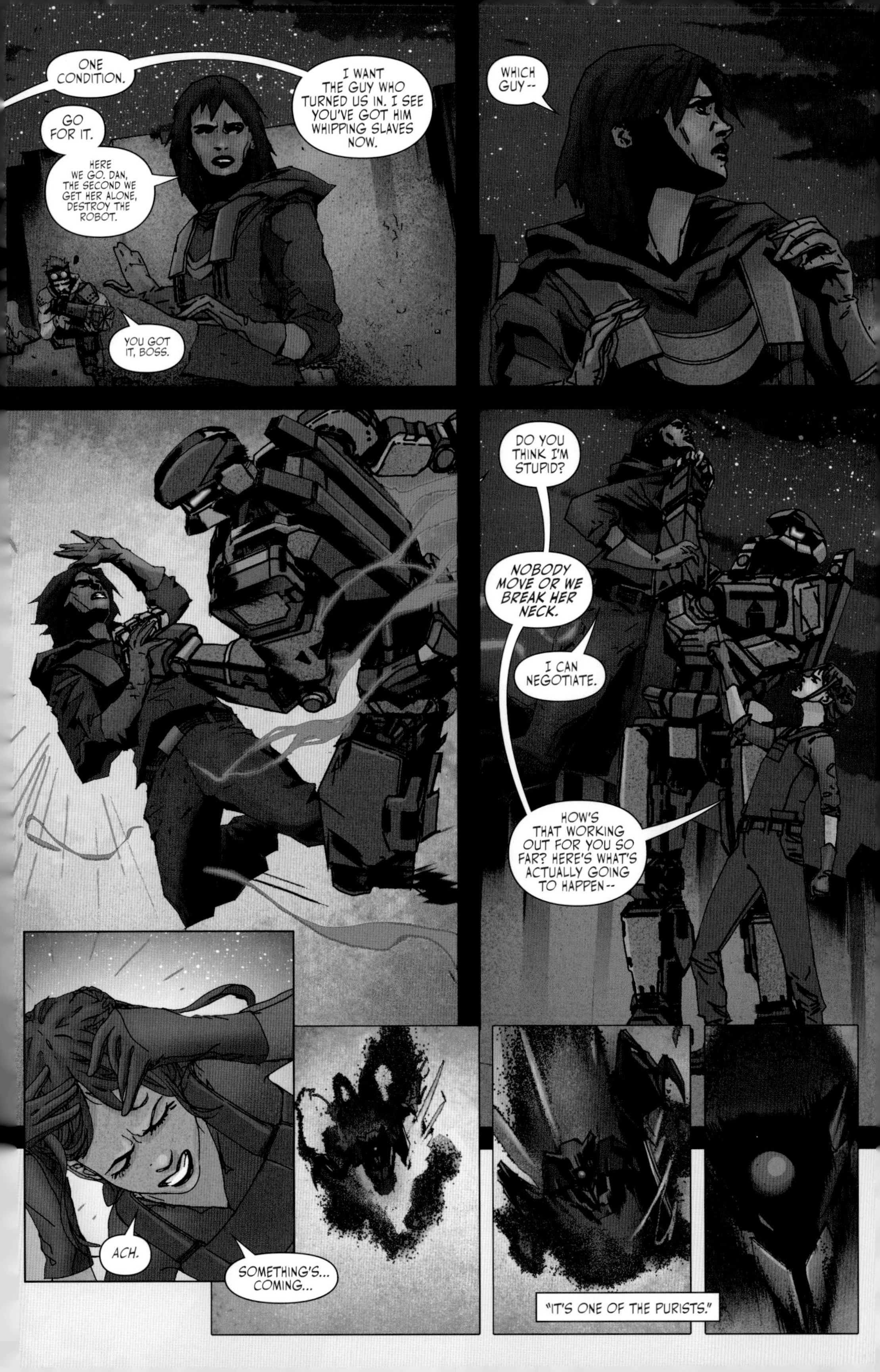
ONE CONDITION.
I WANT THE GUY WHO TURNED US IN. I SEE YOU'VE GOT HIM WHIPPING SLAVES NOW.
GO FOR IT.
HERE WE GO. DAN, THE SECOND WE GET HER ALONE, DESTROY THE ROBOT.
YOU GOT IT, BOSS.
WHICH GUY --
DO YOU THINK I'M STUPID?
NOBODY MOVE OR WE BREAK HER NECK.
I CAN NEGOTIATE.
HOW'S THAT WORKING OUT FOR YOU SO FAR? HERE'S WHAT'S ACTUALLY GOING TO HAPPEN--
ACH.
SOMETHING'S... COMING...
"IT'S ONE OF THE PURISTS."

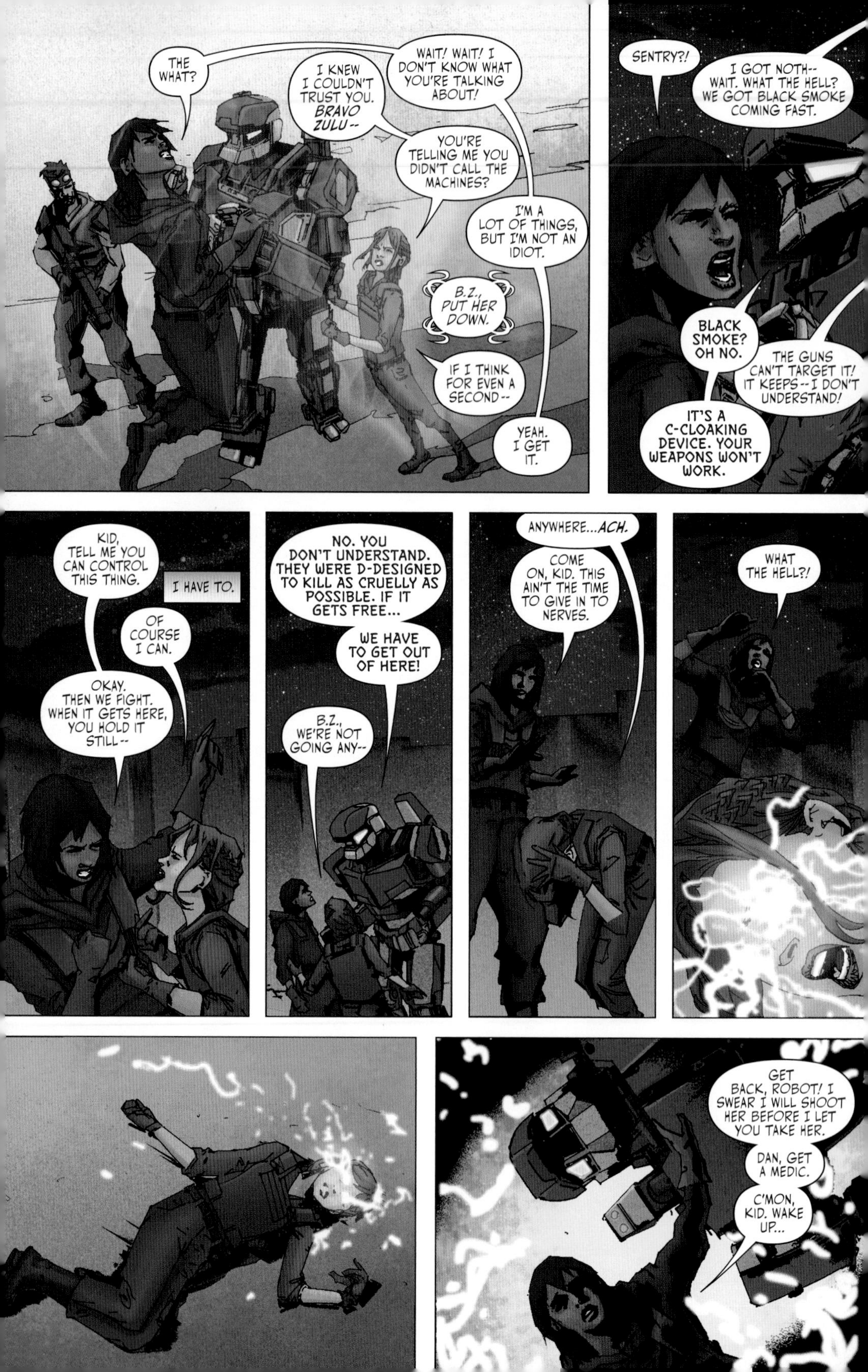
THE WHAT?
I KNEW I COULDN'T TRUST YOU. *BRAVO ZULU* --
WAIT! WAIT! I DON'T KNOW WHAT YOU'RE TALKING ABOUT!
YOU'RE TELLING ME YOU DIDN'T CALL THE MACHINES?
I'M A LOT OF THINGS, BUT I'M NOT AN IDIOT.
B.Z., PUT HER DOWN.
IF I THINK FOR EVEN A SECOND--
YEAH. I GET IT.
SENTRY?!
I GOT NOTH-- WAIT. WHAT THE HELL? WE GOT BLACK SMOKE COMING FAST.
BLACK SMOKE? OH NO.
THE GUNS CAN'T TARGET IT! IT KEEPS--I DON'T UNDERSTAND!
IT'S A C-CLOAKING DEVICE. YOUR WEAPONS WON'T WORK.
KID, TELL ME YOU CAN CONTROL THIS THING.
I HAVE TO.
OF COURSE I CAN.
OKAY. THEN WE FIGHT. WHEN IT GETS HERE, YOU HOLD IT STILL--
NO. YOU DON'T UNDERSTAND. THEY WERE D-DESIGNED TO KILL AS CRUELLY AS POSSIBLE. IF IT GETS FREE...
WE HAVE TO GET OUT OF HERE!
B.Z., WE'RE NOT GOING ANY--
ANYWHERE...*ACH.*
COME ON, KID. THIS AIN'T THE TIME TO GIVE IN TO NERVES.
WHAT THE HELL?!
GET BACK, ROBOT! I SWEAR I WILL SHOOT HER BEFORE I LET YOU TAKE HER.
DAN, GET A MEDIC.
C'MON, KID. WAKE UP...

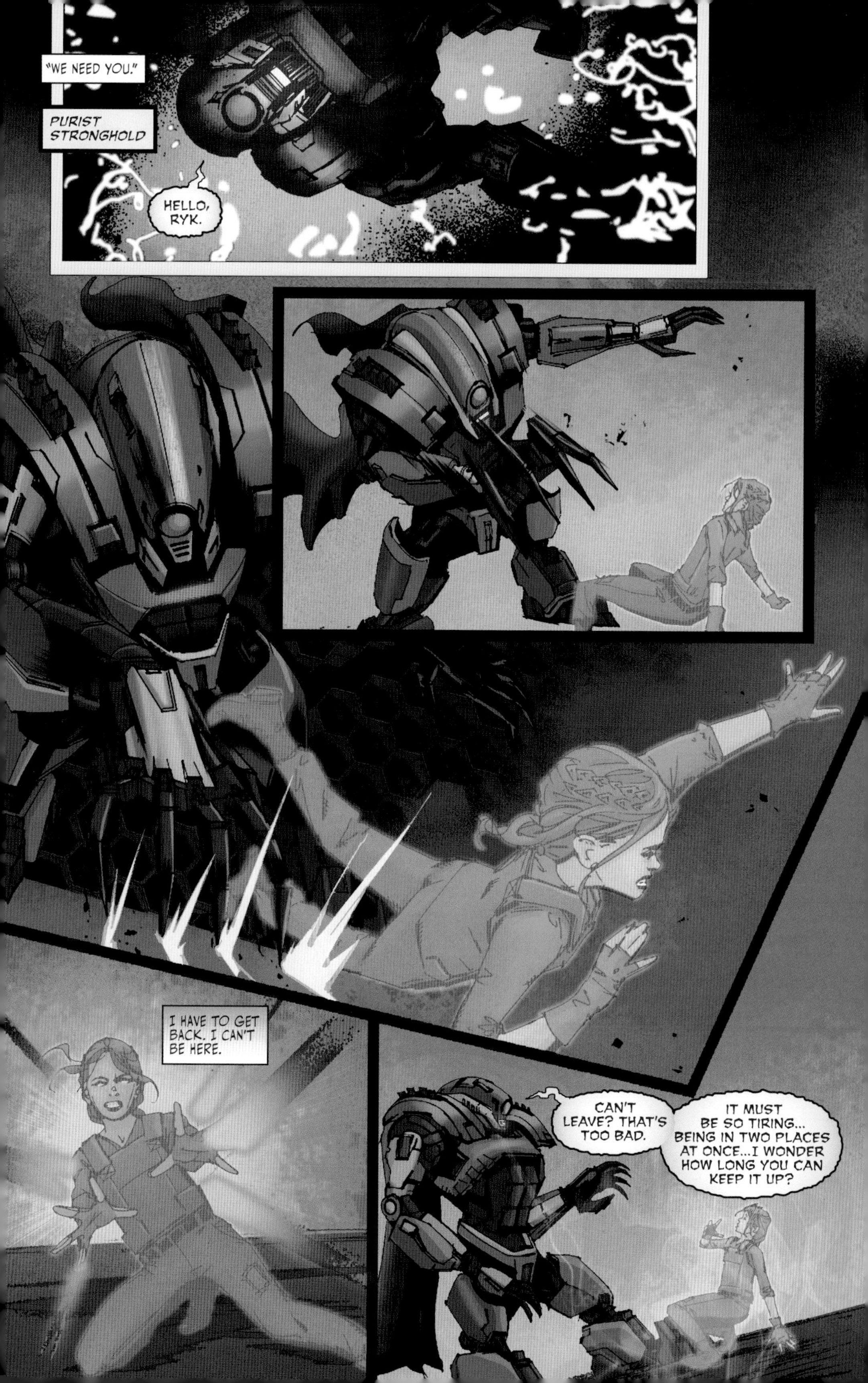
"WE NEED YOU."
PURIST STRONGHOLD
HELLO, RYK.
I HAVE TO GET BACK. I CAN'T BE HERE.
CAN'T LEAVE? THAT'S TOO BAD.
IT MUST BE SO TIRING... BEING IN TWO PLACES AT ONCE...I WONDER HOW LONG YOU CAN KEEP IT UP?

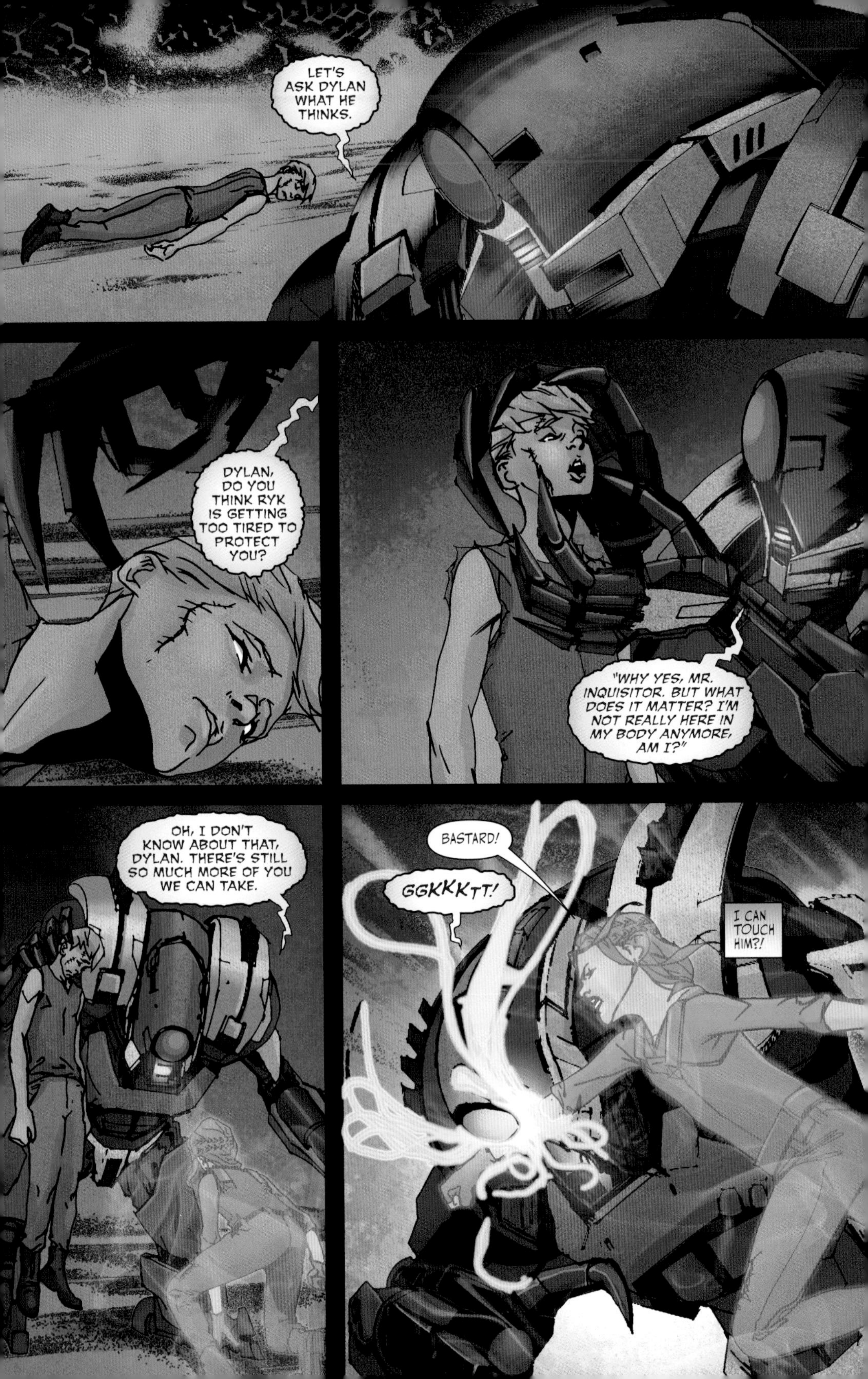
LET'S ASK DYLAN WHAT HE THINKS.
DYLAN, DO YOU THINK RYK IS GETTING TOO TIRED TO PROTECT YOU?
"WHY YES, MR. INQUISITOR. BUT WHAT DOES IT MATTER? I'M NOT REALLY HERE IN MY BODY ANYMORE, AM I?"
OH, I DON'T KNOW ABOUT THAT, DYLAN. THERE'S STILL SO MUCH MORE OF YOU WE CAN TAKE.
BASTARD!
GGKKKTT!
I CAN TOUCH HIM?!

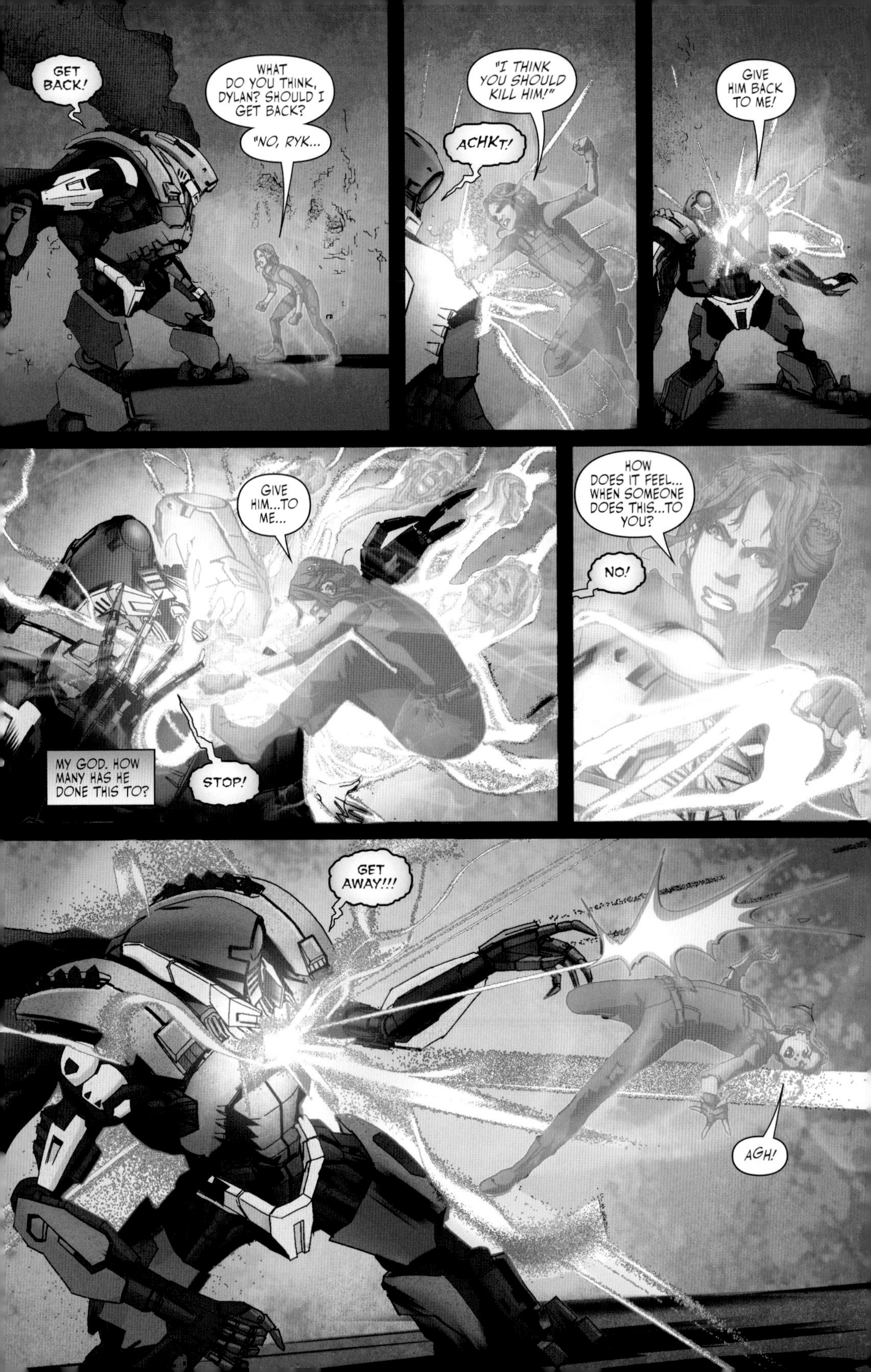
GET BACK!
WHAT DO YOU THINK, DYLAN? SHOULD I GET BACK?
"NO, RYK...
"I THINK YOU SHOULD KILL HIM!"
ACHKT!
GIVE HIM BACK TO ME!
GIVE HIM...TO ME...
MY GOD. HOW MANY HAS HE DONE THIS TO?
STOP!
HOW DOES IT FEEL... WHEN SOMEONE DOES THIS...TO YOU?
NO!
GET AWAY!!!
AGH!

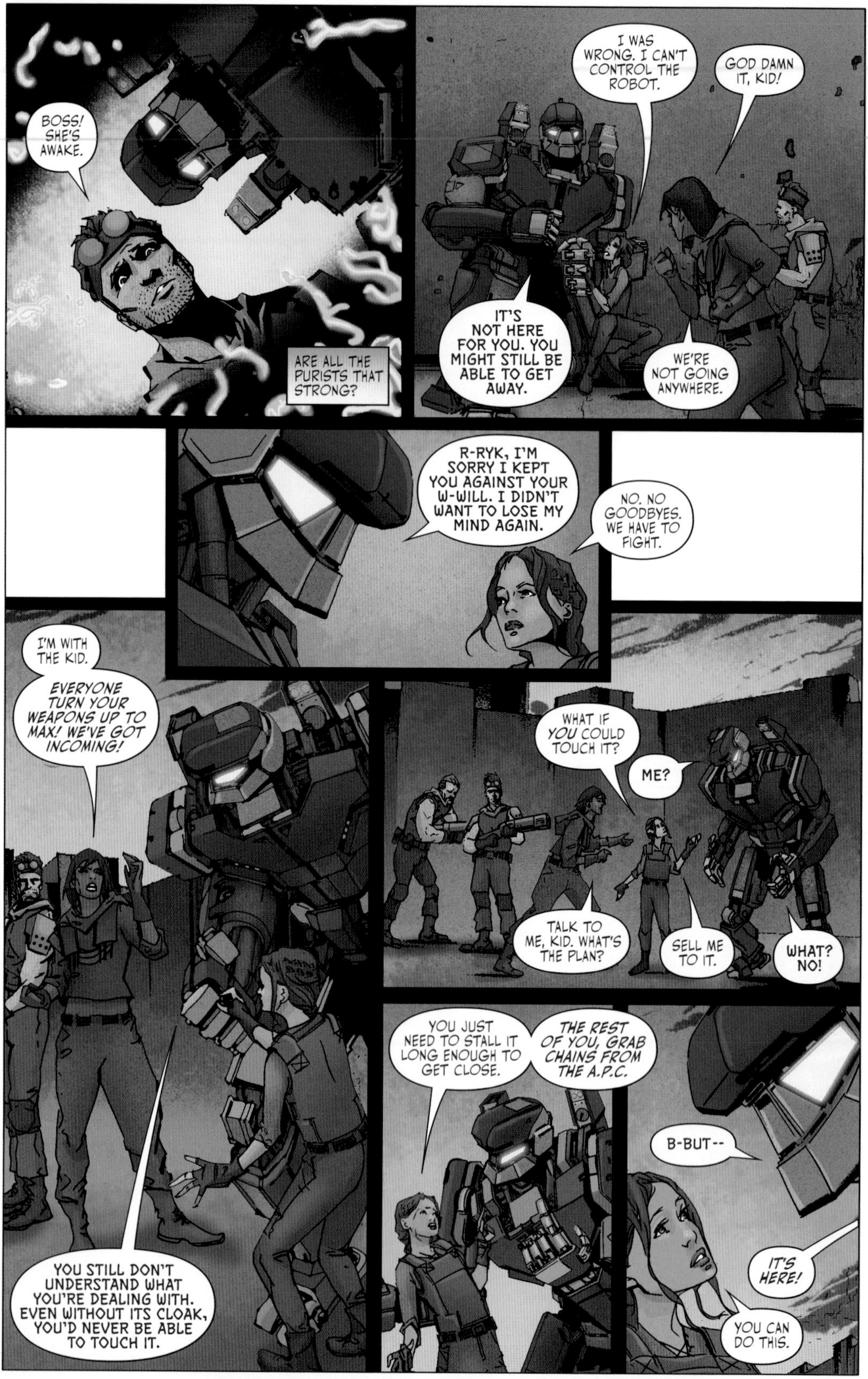
BOSS! SHE'S AWAKE.
ARE ALL THE PURISTS THAT STRONG?
I WAS WRONG. I CAN'T CONTROL THE ROBOT.
GOD DAMN IT, KID!
IT'S NOT HERE FOR YOU. YOU MIGHT STILL BE ABLE TO GET AWAY.
WE'RE NOT GOING ANYWHERE.
R-RYK, I'M SORRY I KEPT YOU AGAINST YOUR W-WILL. I DIDN'T WANT TO LOSE MY MIND AGAIN.
NO. NO GOODBYES. WE HAVE TO FIGHT.
I'M WITH THE KID.
EVERYONE TURN YOUR WEAPONS UP TO MAX! WE'VE GOT INCOMING!
YOU STILL DON'T UNDERSTAND WHAT YOU'RE DEALING WITH. EVEN WITHOUT ITS CLOAK, YOU'D NEVER BE ABLE TO TOUCH IT.
WHAT IF YOU COULD TOUCH IT?
ME?
TALK TO ME, KID. WHAT'S THE PLAN?
SELL ME TO IT.
WHAT? NO!
YOU JUST NEED TO STALL IT LONG ENOUGH TO GET CLOSE.
THE REST OF YOU, GRAB CHAINS FROM THE A.P.C.
B-BUT--
IT'S HERE!
YOU CAN DO THIS.

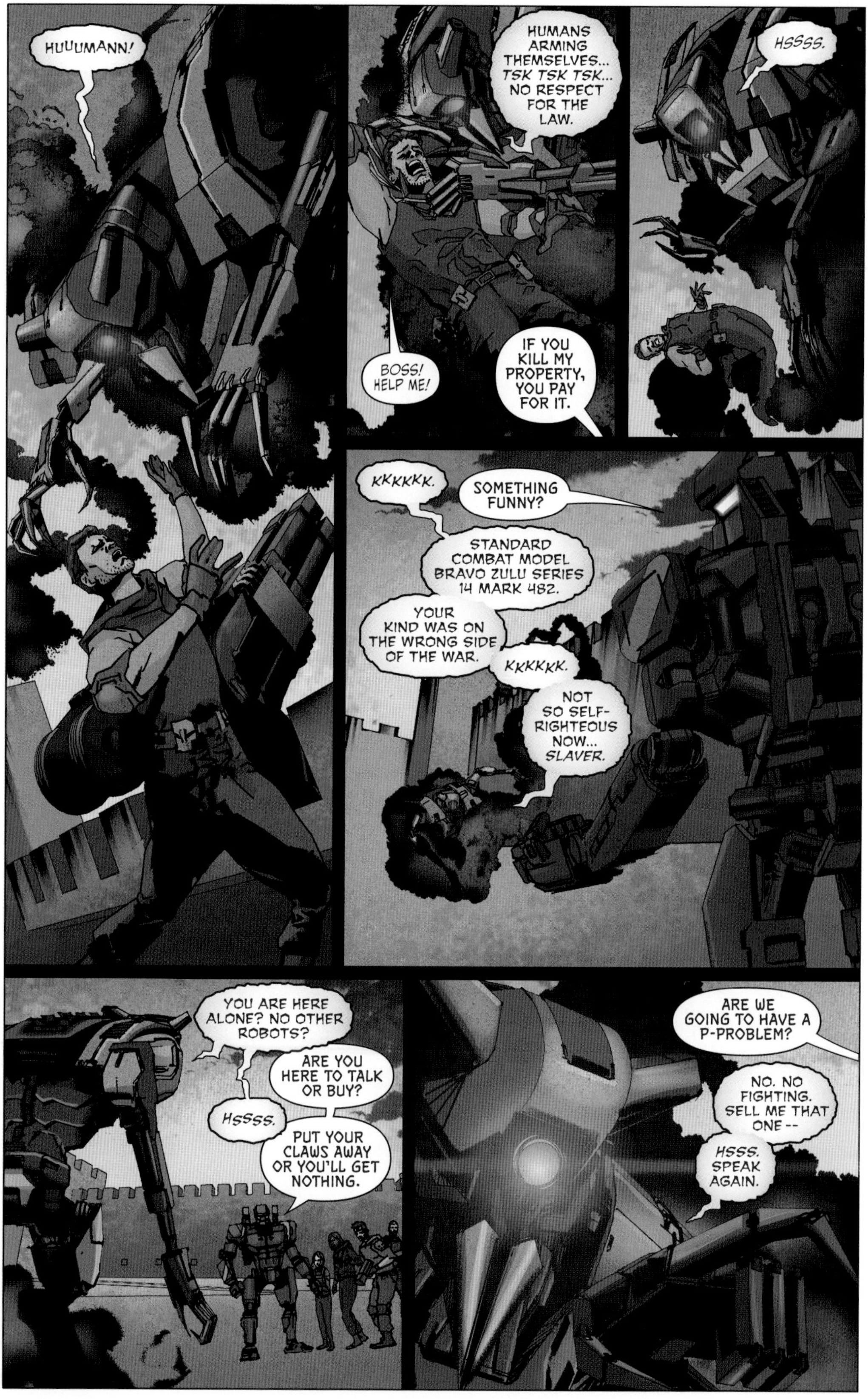
HUUUMANN!
HUMANS ARMING THEMSELVES... TSK TSK TSK... NO RESPECT FOR THE LAW.
BOSS! HELP ME!
IF YOU KILL MY PROPERTY, YOU PAY FOR IT.
HSSSS.
KKKKKK.
SOMETHING FUNNY?
STANDARD COMBAT MODEL BRAVO ZULU SERIES 14 MARK 482.
YOUR KIND WAS ON THE WRONG SIDE OF THE WAR.
KKKKKK.
NOT SO SELF-RIGHTEOUS NOW... SLAVER.
YOU ARE HERE ALONE? NO OTHER ROBOTS?
ARE YOU HERE TO TALK OR BUY?
HSSSS.
PUT YOUR CLAWS AWAY OR YOU'LL GET NOTHING.
ARE WE GOING TO HAVE A P-PROBLEM?
NO. NO FIGHTING. SELL ME THAT ONE --
HSSS. SPEAK AGAIN.

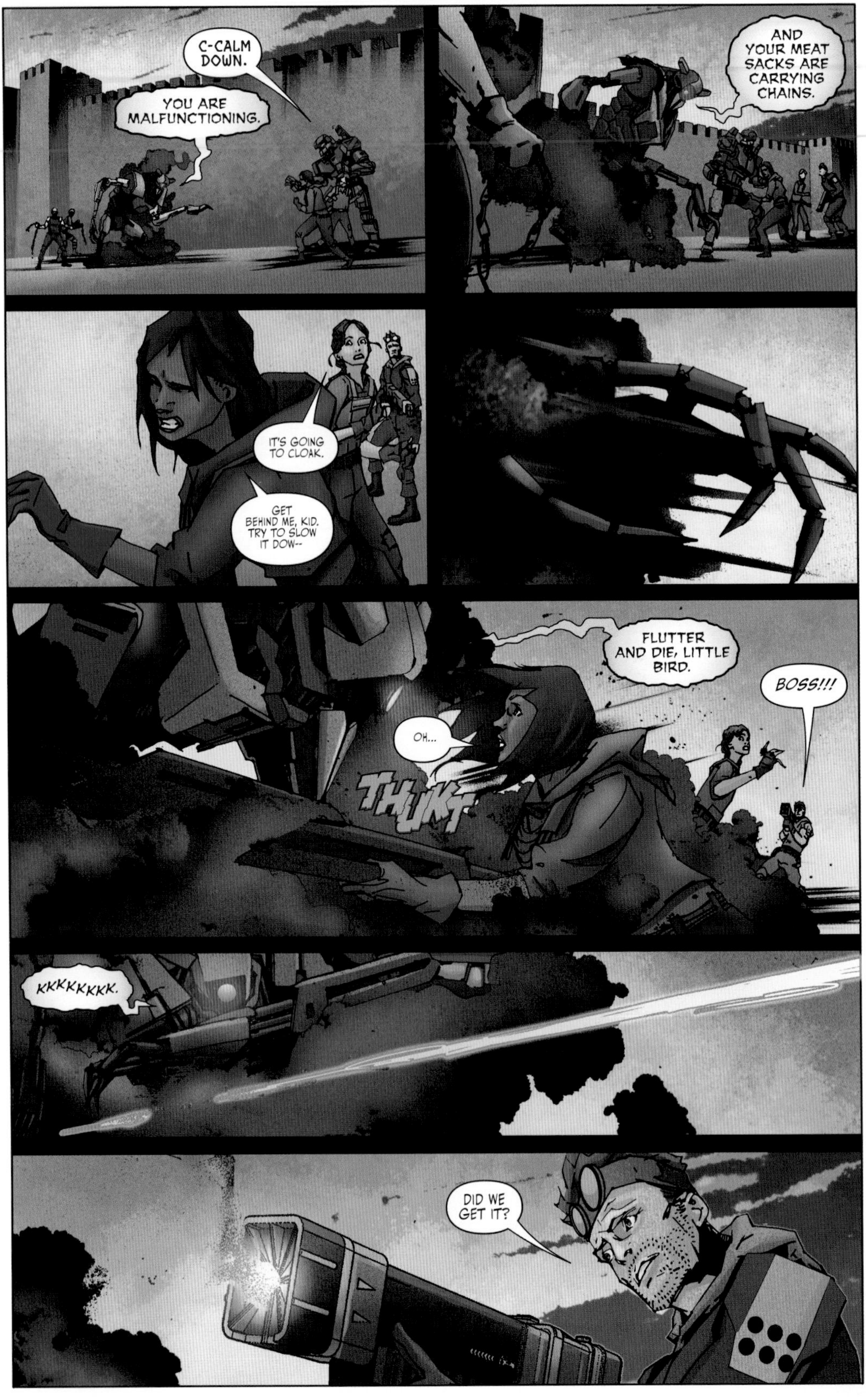
C-CALM DOWN.
YOU ARE MALFUNCTIONING.
AND YOUR MEAT SACKS ARE CARRYING CHAINS.
IT'S GOING TO CLOAK.
GET BEHIND ME, KID. TRY TO SLOW IT DOW--
FLUTTER AND DIE, LITTLE BIRD.
BOSS!!!
OH...
THUNK
KKKKKKKK.
DID WE GET IT?

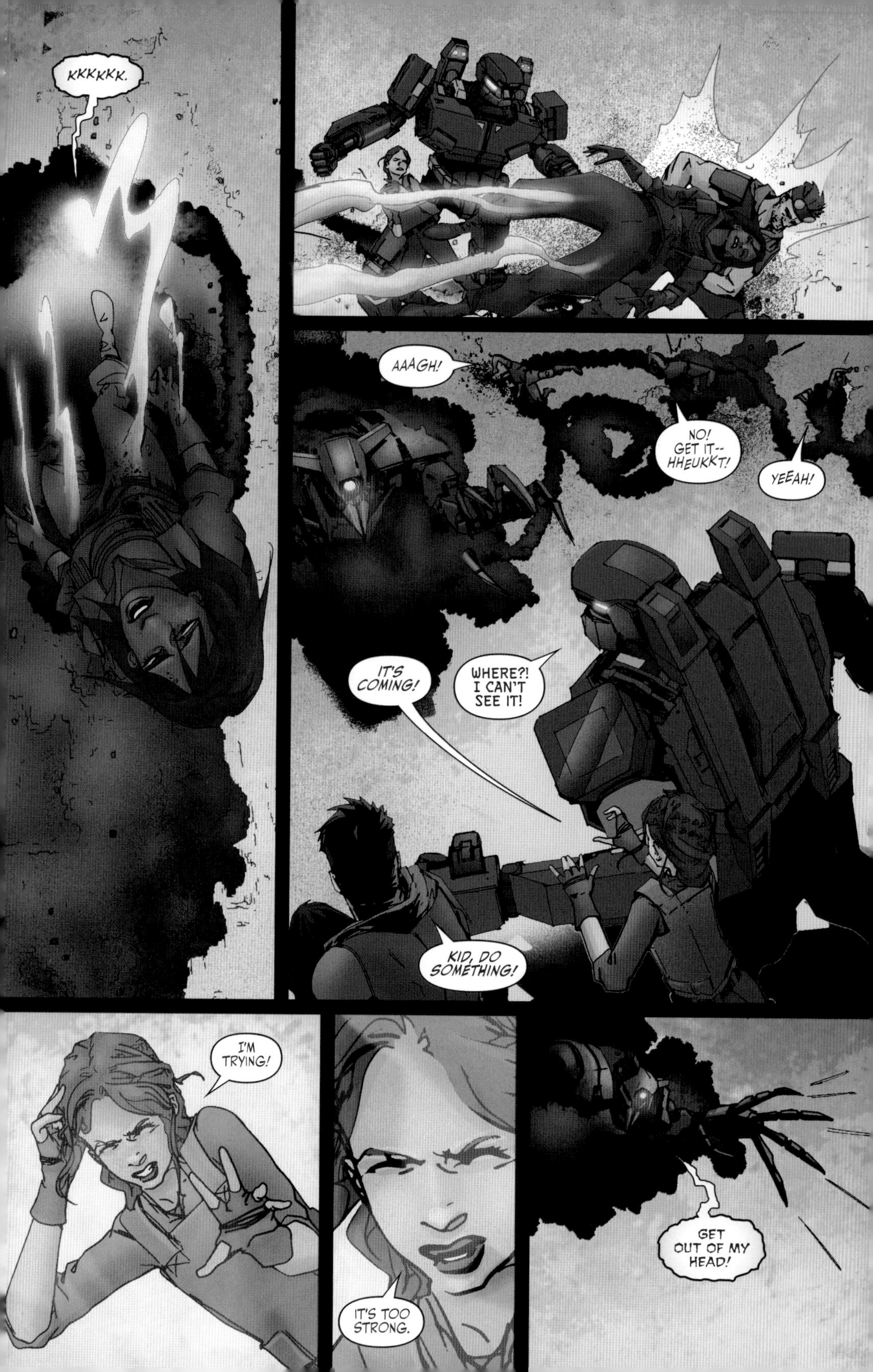
KKKKKK.
AAAGH!
NO! GET IT-- HHEUKKT!
YEEAH!
IT'S COMING!
WHERE?! I CAN'T SEE IT!
KID, DO SOMETHING!
I'M TRYING!
IT'S TOO STRONG.
GET OUT OF MY HEAD!

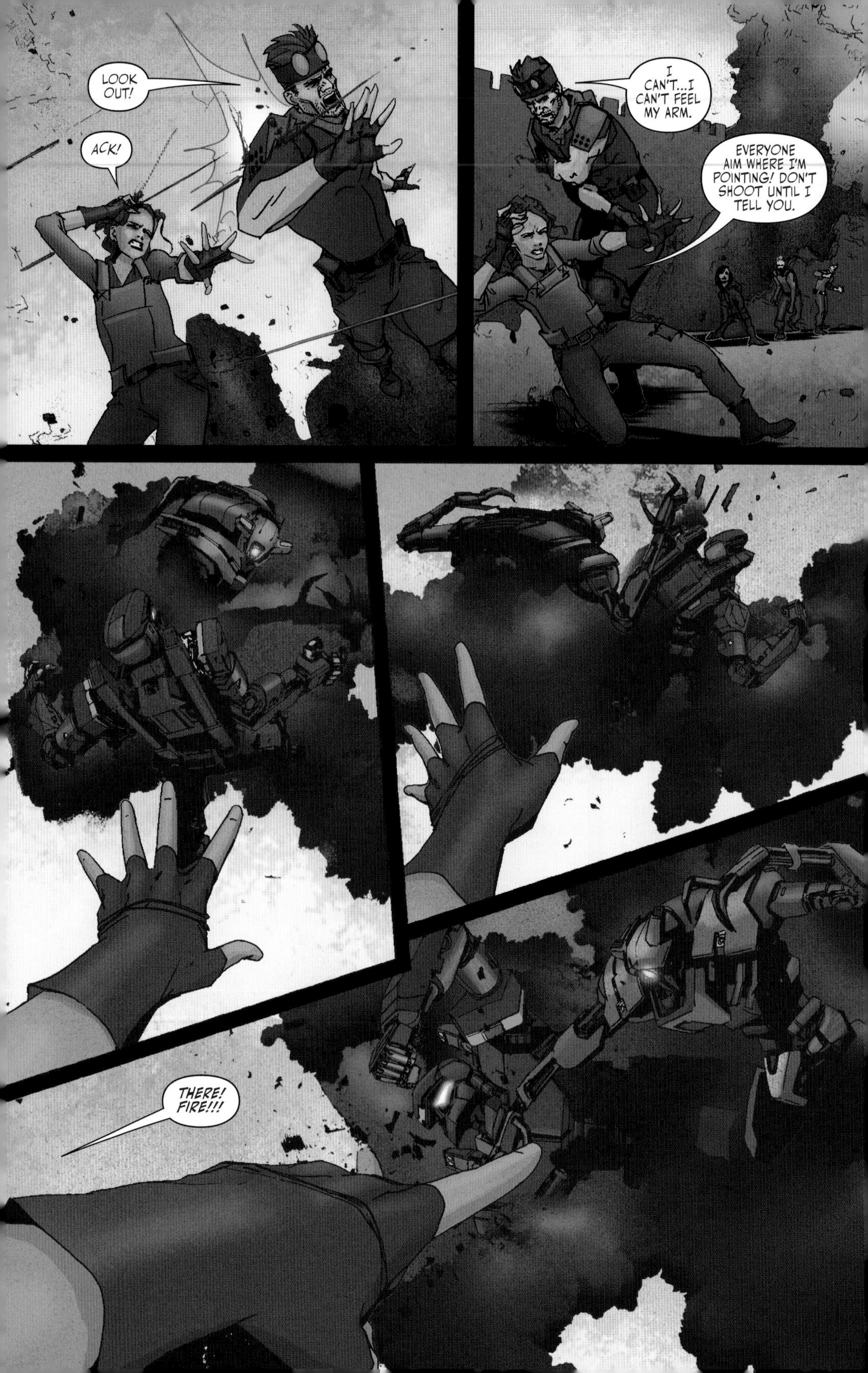
LOOK OUT!
ACK!
I CAN'T...I CAN'T FEEL MY ARM.
EVERYONE AIM WHERE I'M POINTING! DON'T SHOOT UNTIL I TELL YOU.
THERE! FIRE!!!

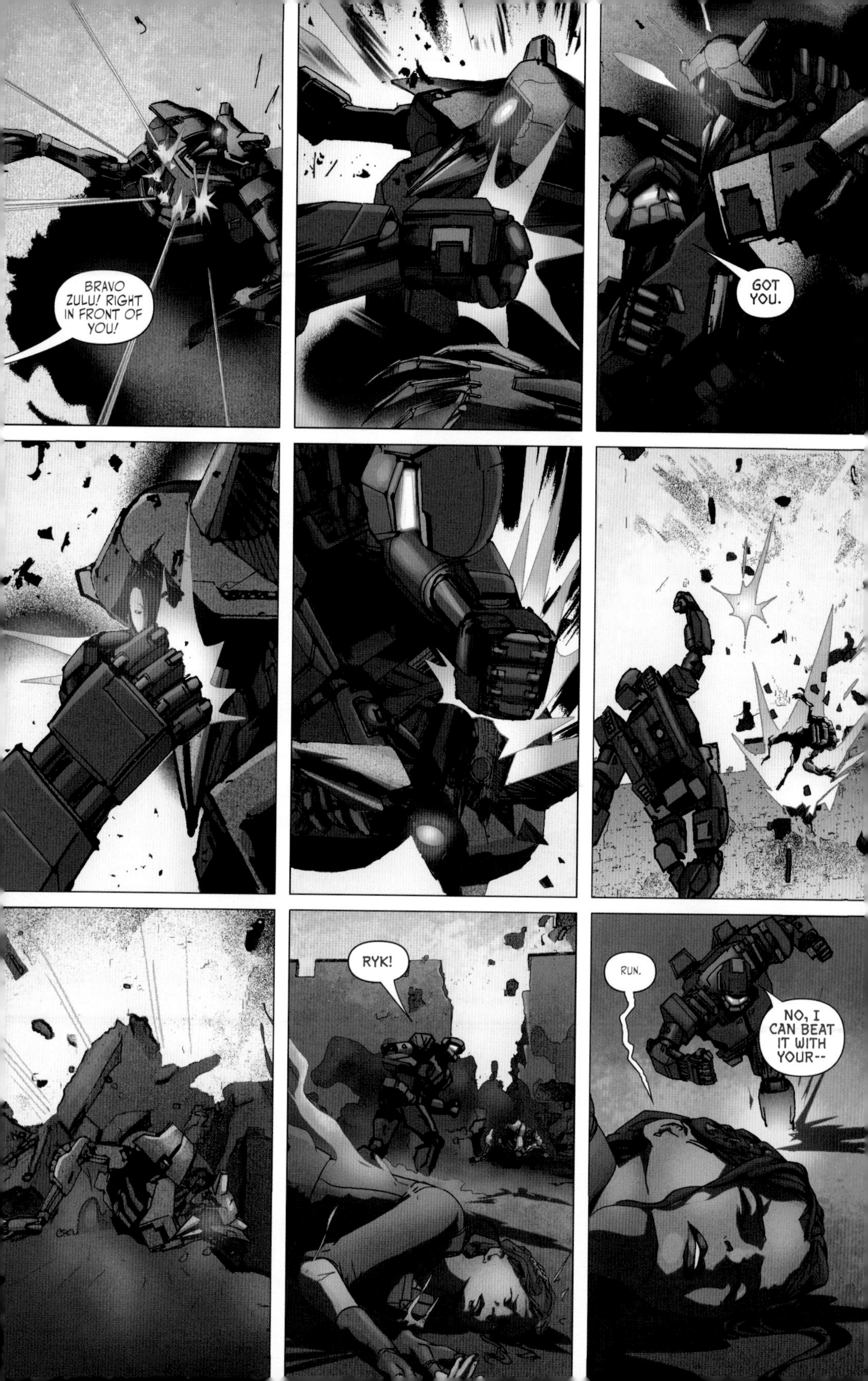
BRAVO ZULU! RIGHT IN FRONT OF YOU!
GOT YOU.
RYK!
RUN.
NO, I CAN BEAT IT WITH YOUR--

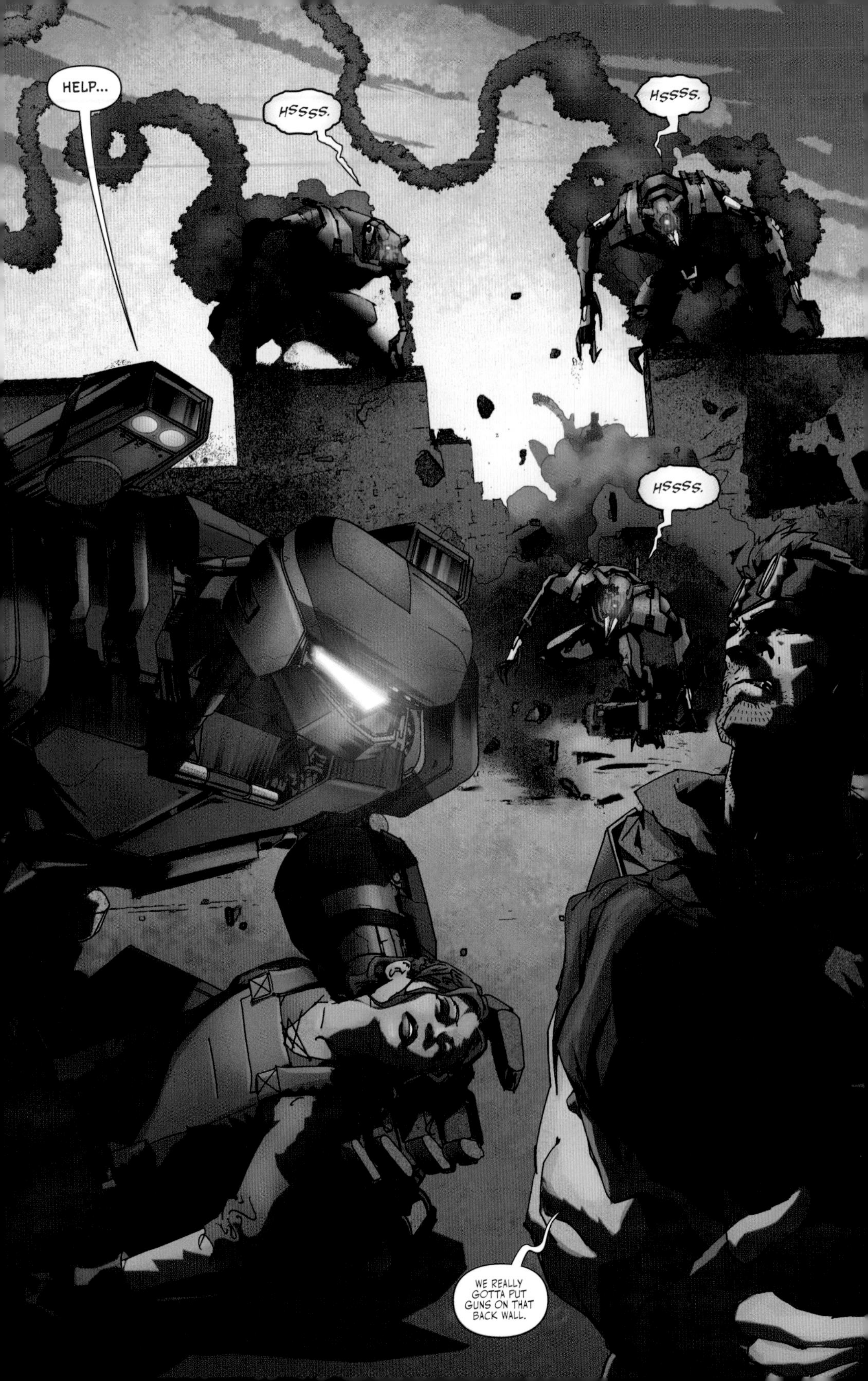
HELP...
HSSSS.
HSSSS.
HSSSS.
WE REALLY GOTTA PUT GUNS ON THAT BACK WALL.

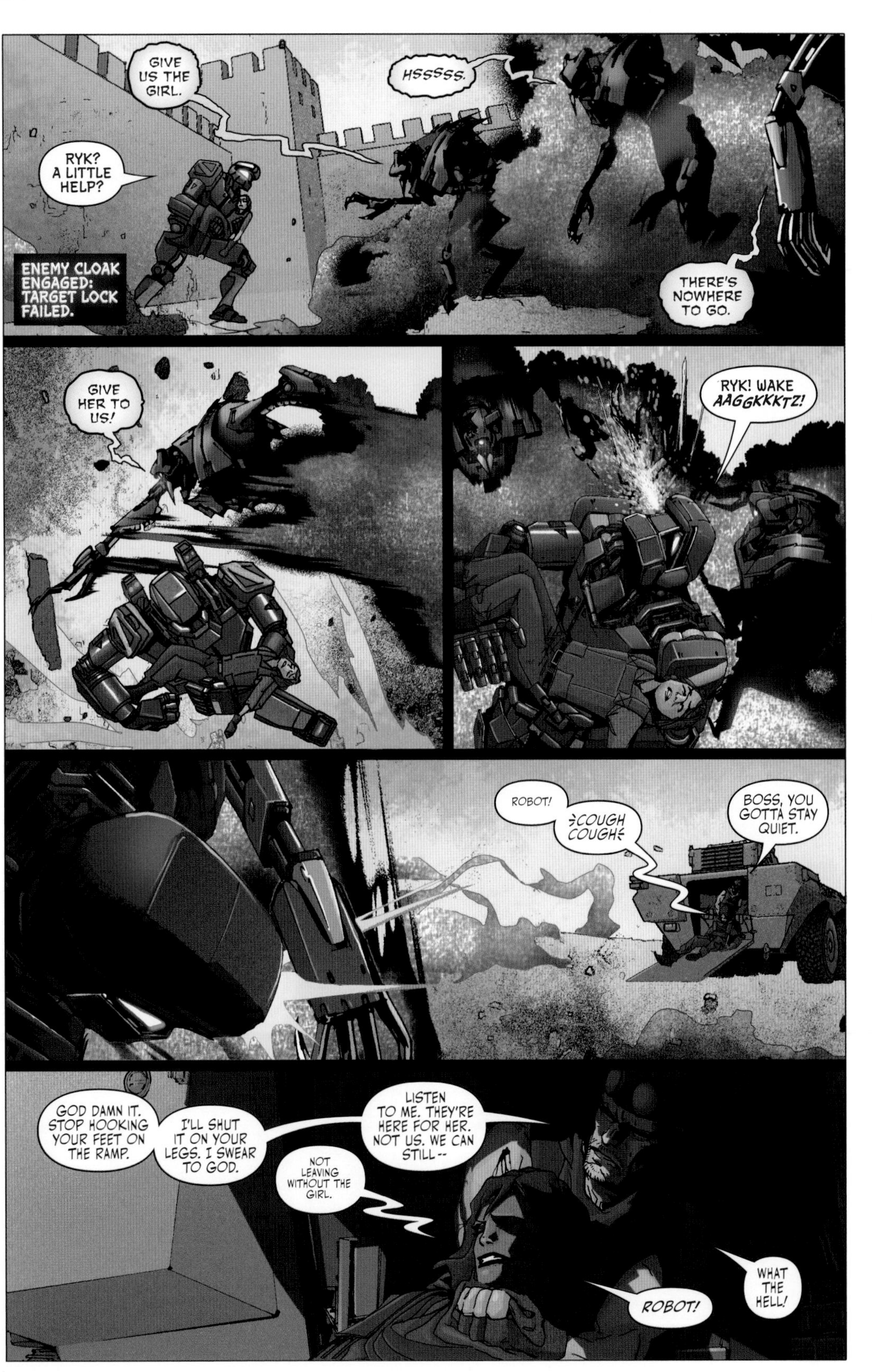
GIVE US THE GIRL.
HSSSSS.
RYK? A LITTLE HELP?
ENEMY CLOAK ENGAGED: TARGET LOCK FAILED.
THERE'S NOWHERE TO GO.
GIVE HER TO US!
RYK! WAKE AAGGKKKTZ!
ROBOT!
COUGH COUGH
BOSS, YOU GOTTA STAY QUIET.
GOD DAMN IT. STOP HOOKING YOUR FEET ON THE RAMP.
I'LL SHUT IT ON YOUR LEGS. I SWEAR TO GOD.
LISTEN TO ME. THEY'RE HERE FOR HER. NOT US. WE CAN STILL--
NOT LEAVING WITHOUT THE GIRL.
WHAT THE HELL!
ROBOT!

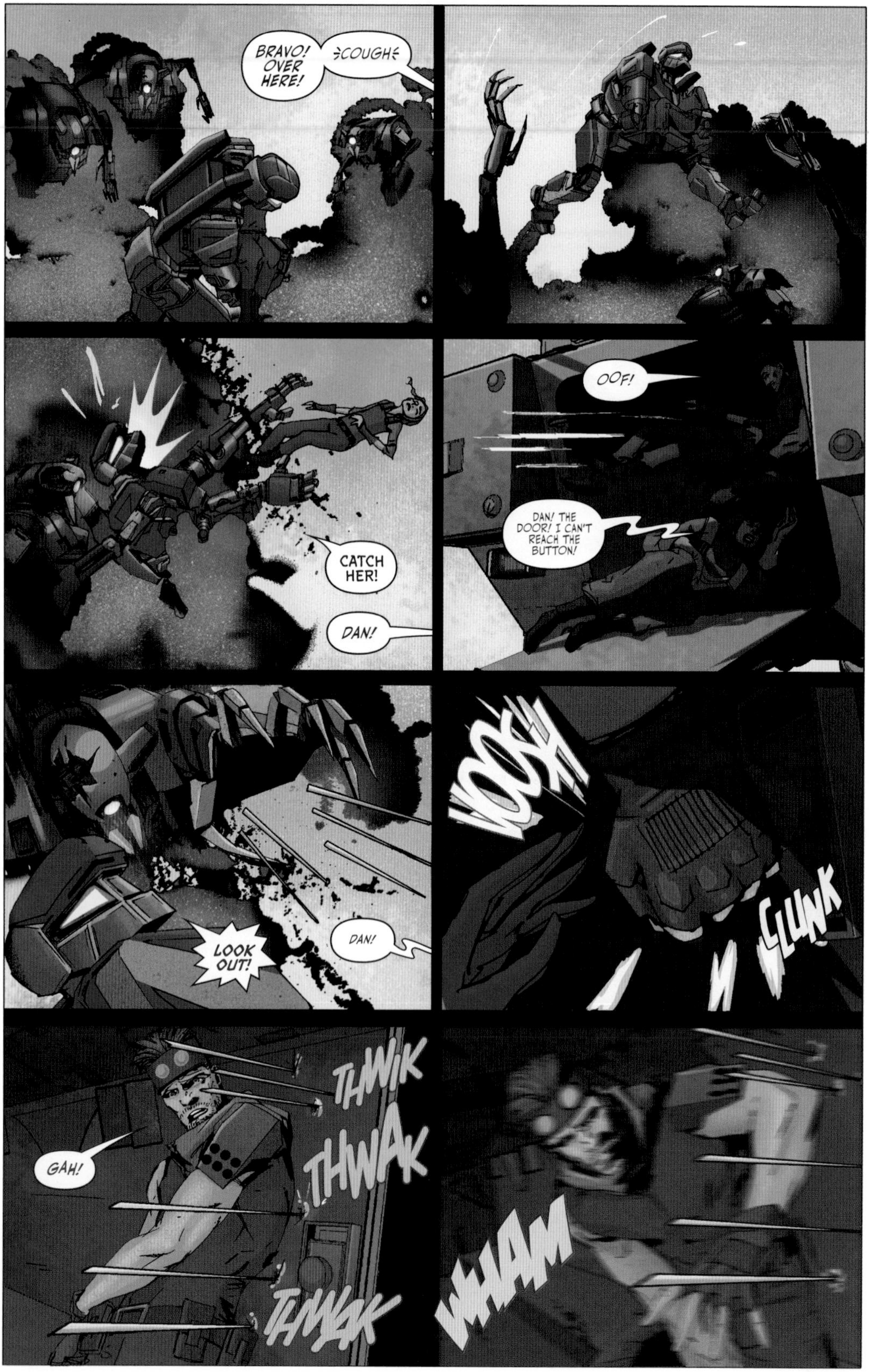
BRAVO! OVER HERE!
>COUGH<
CATCH HER!
DAN!
OOF!
DAN! THE DOOR! I CAN'T REACH THE BUTTON!
LOOK OUT!
DAN!
WOOSH!
CLUNK
GAH!
THWIK
THWAK
THWAK
WHAM

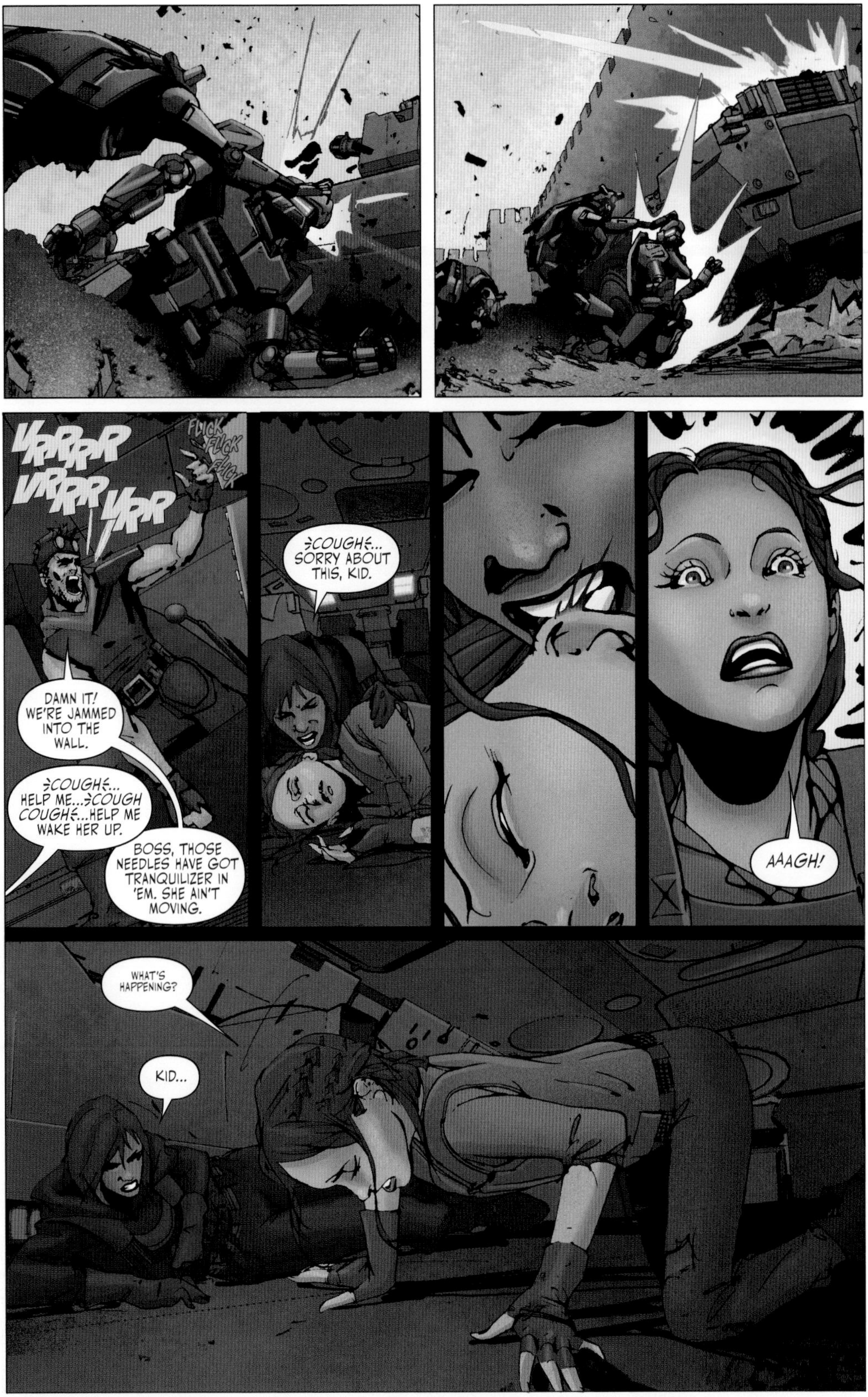
VRRRR VRRRR VRRR
FLICK FLICK FLICK
DAMN IT! WE'RE JAMMED INTO THE WALL.
≥COUGH≤... HELP ME...≥COUGH COUGH≤...HELP ME WAKE HER UP.
BOSS, THOSE NEEDLES HAVE GOT TRANQUILIZER IN 'EM. SHE AIN'T MOVING.
≥COUGH≤... SORRY ABOUT THIS, KID.
AAAGH!
WHAT'S HAPPENING?
KID...

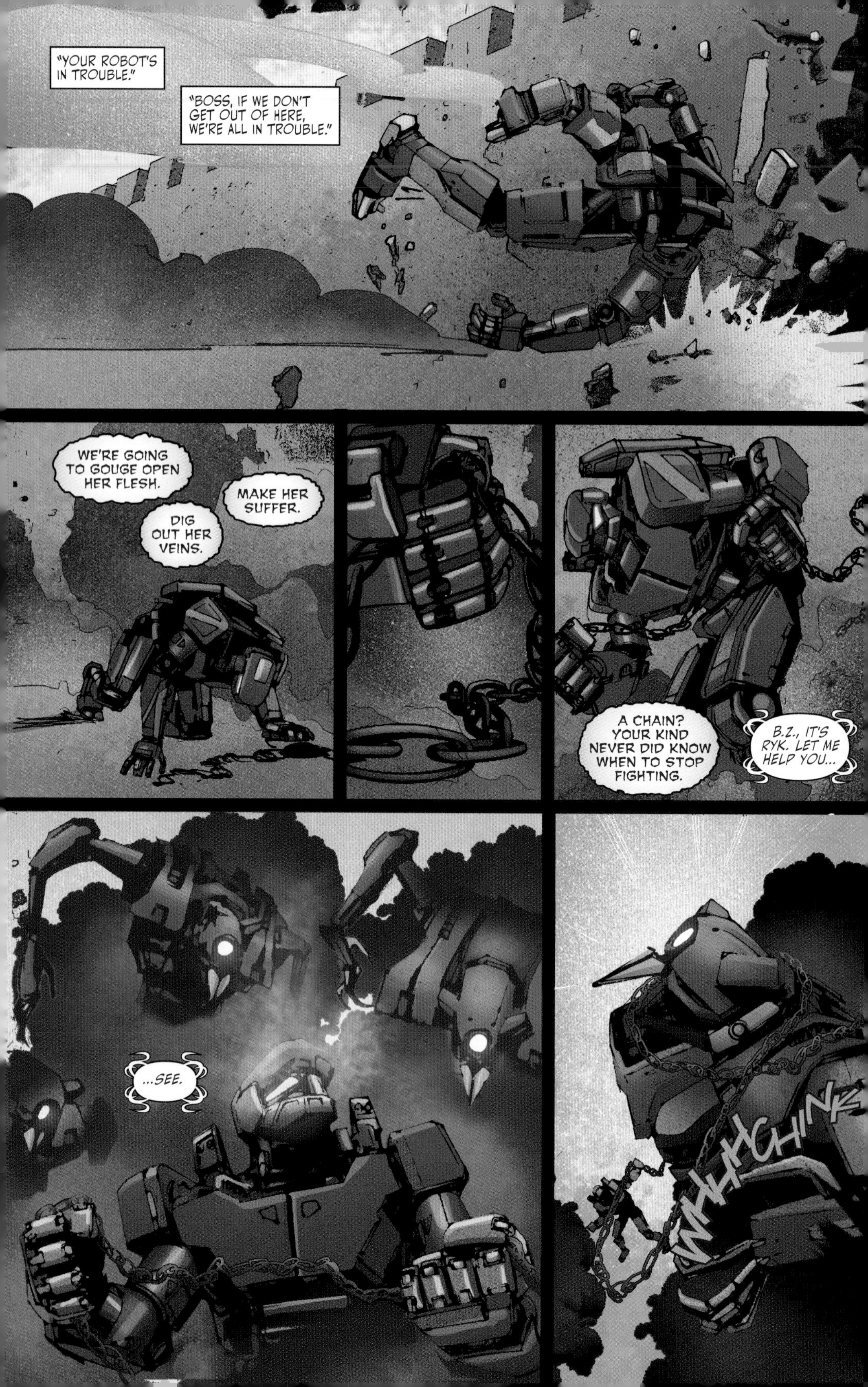
"YOUR ROBOT'S IN TROUBLE."
"BOSS, IF WE DON'T GET OUT OF HERE, WE'RE ALL IN TROUBLE."
WE'RE GOING TO GOUGE OPEN HER FLESH.
DIG OUT HER VEINS.
MAKE HER SUFFER.
A CHAIN? YOUR KIND NEVER DID KNOW WHEN TO STOP FIGHTING.
B.Z., IT'S RYK. LET ME HELP YOU...
...SEE.
WHHCHINK

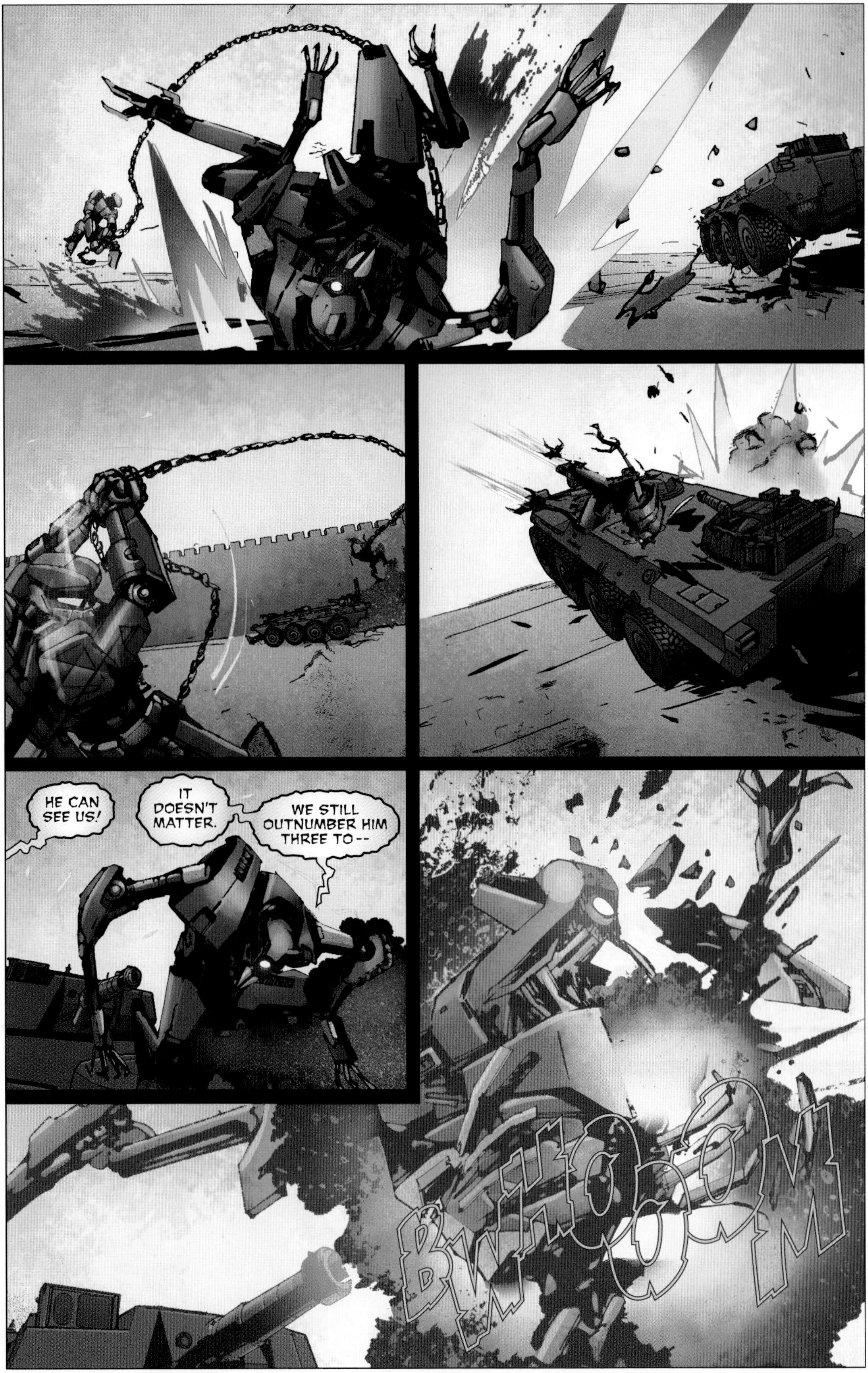
HE CAN SEE US!
IT DOESN'T MATTER.
WE STILL OUTNUMBER HIM THREE TO--
BWHOOOOM

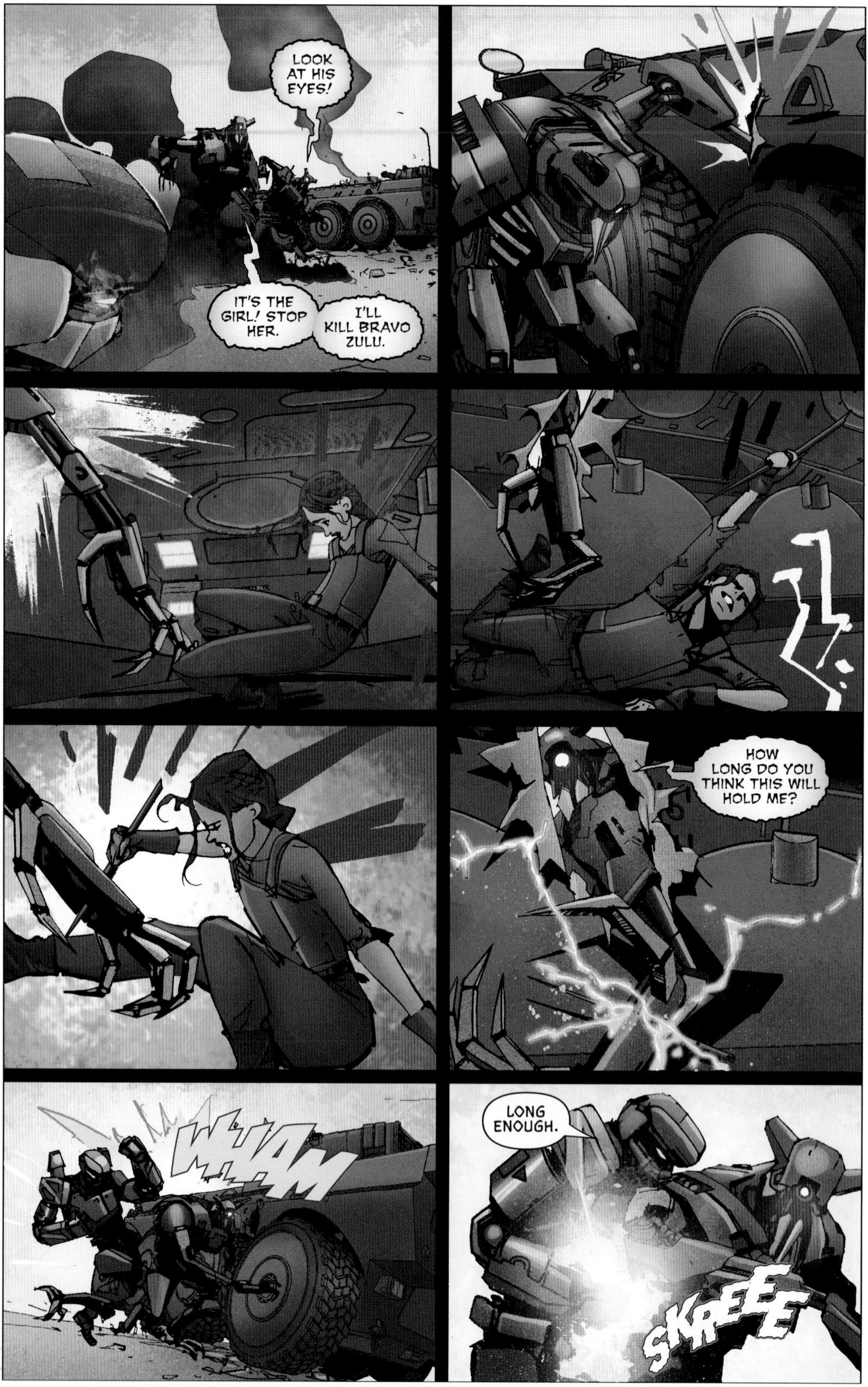
LOOK AT HIS EYES!
IT'S THE GIRL! STOP HER.
I'LL KILL BRAVO ZULU.
HOW LONG DO YOU THINK THIS WILL HOLD ME?
WHAM
LONG ENOUGH.
SKREEE

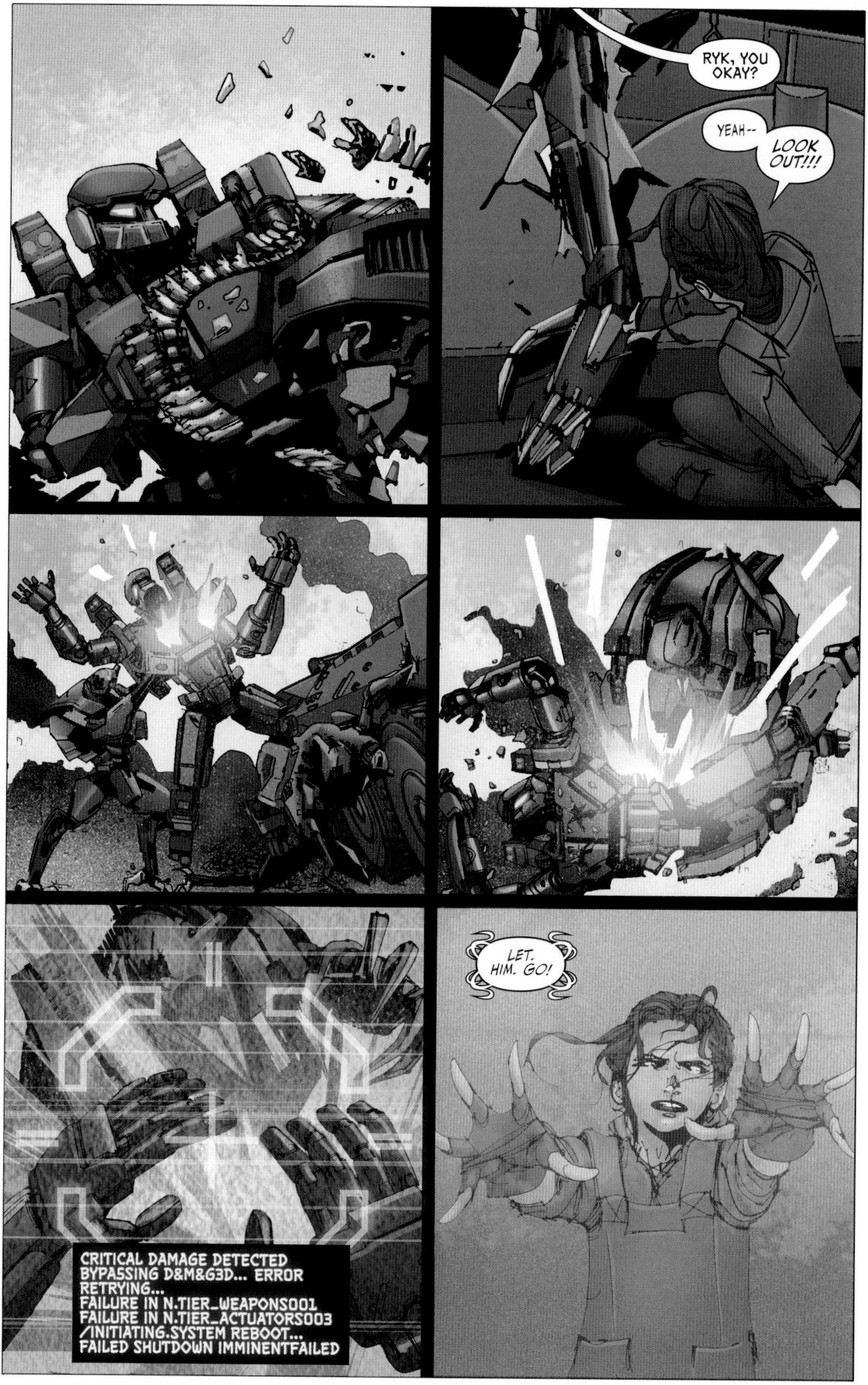
RYK, YOU OKAY?
YEAH--
LOOK OUT!!!
CRITICAL DAMAGE DETECTED
BYPASSING D&M&G3D... ERROR
RETRYING...
FAILURE IN N.TIER_WEAPONS001
FAILURE IN N.TIER_ACTUATORS003
/INITIATING.SYSTEM REBOOT...
FAILED SHUTDOWN IMMINENTFAILED
LET. HIM. GO!

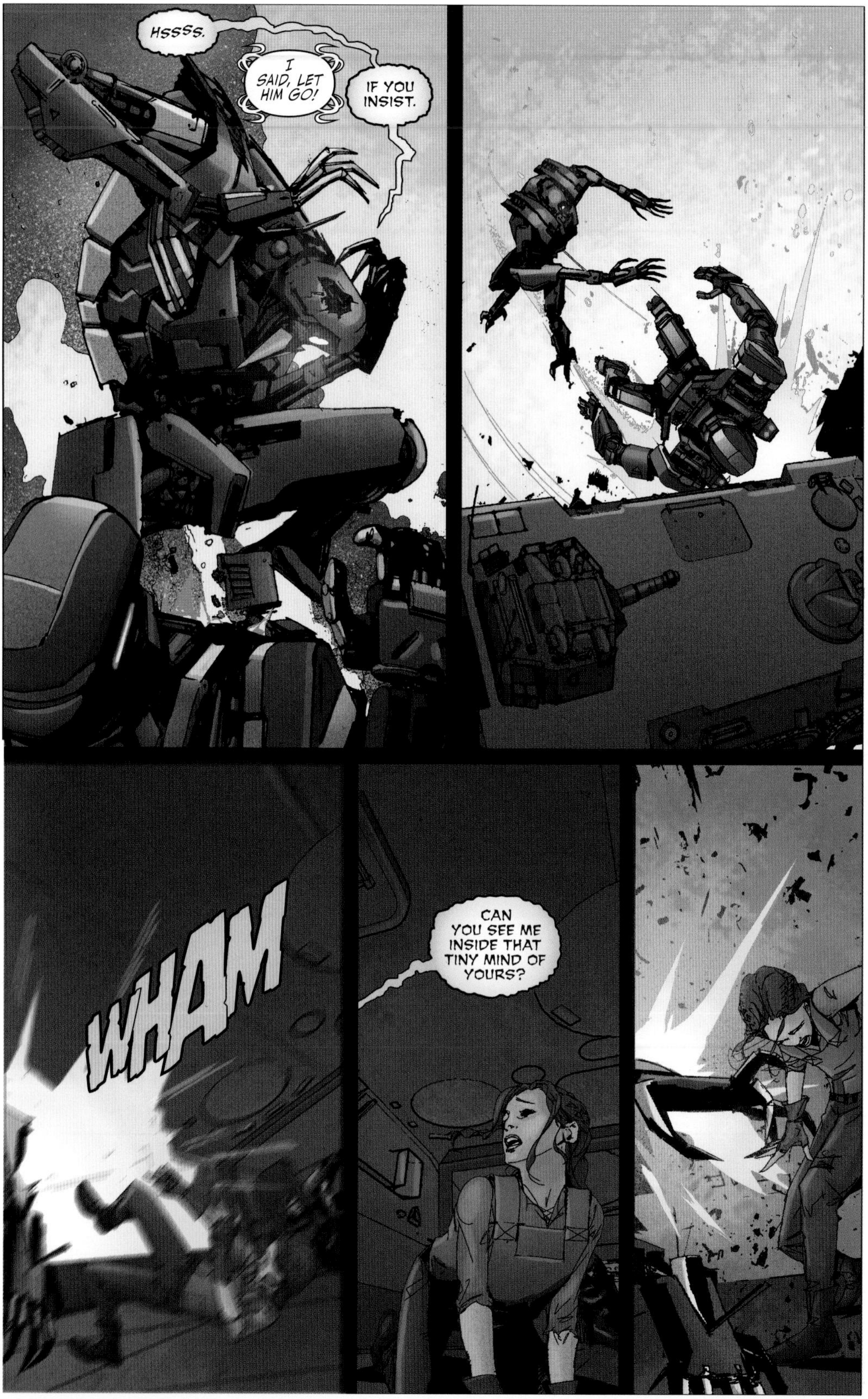
HSSSS.
I SAID, LET HIM GO!
IF YOU INSIST.
WHAM
CAN YOU SEE ME INSIDE THAT TINY MIND OF YOURS?

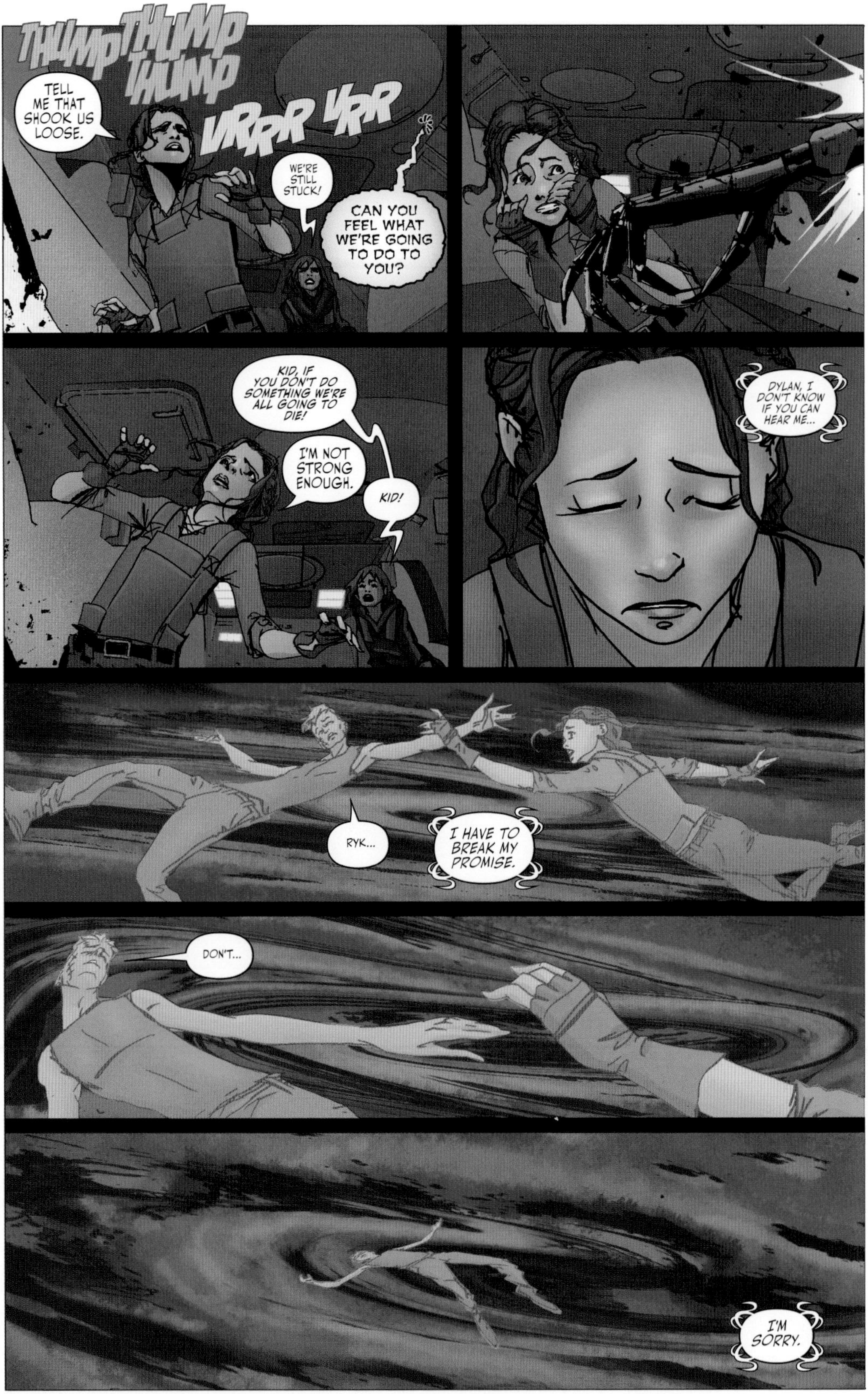
THUMP THUMP THUMP
TELL ME THAT SHOOK US LOOSE.
VRRR VRR
WE'RE STILL STUCK!
CAN YOU FEEL WHAT WE'RE GOING TO DO TO YOU?
KID, IF YOU DON'T DO SOMETHING WE'RE ALL GOING TO DIE!
I'M NOT STRONG ENOUGH.
KID!
DYLAN, I DON'T KNOW IF YOU CAN HEAR ME...
RYK...
I HAVE TO BREAK MY PROMISE.
DON'T...
I'M SORRY.

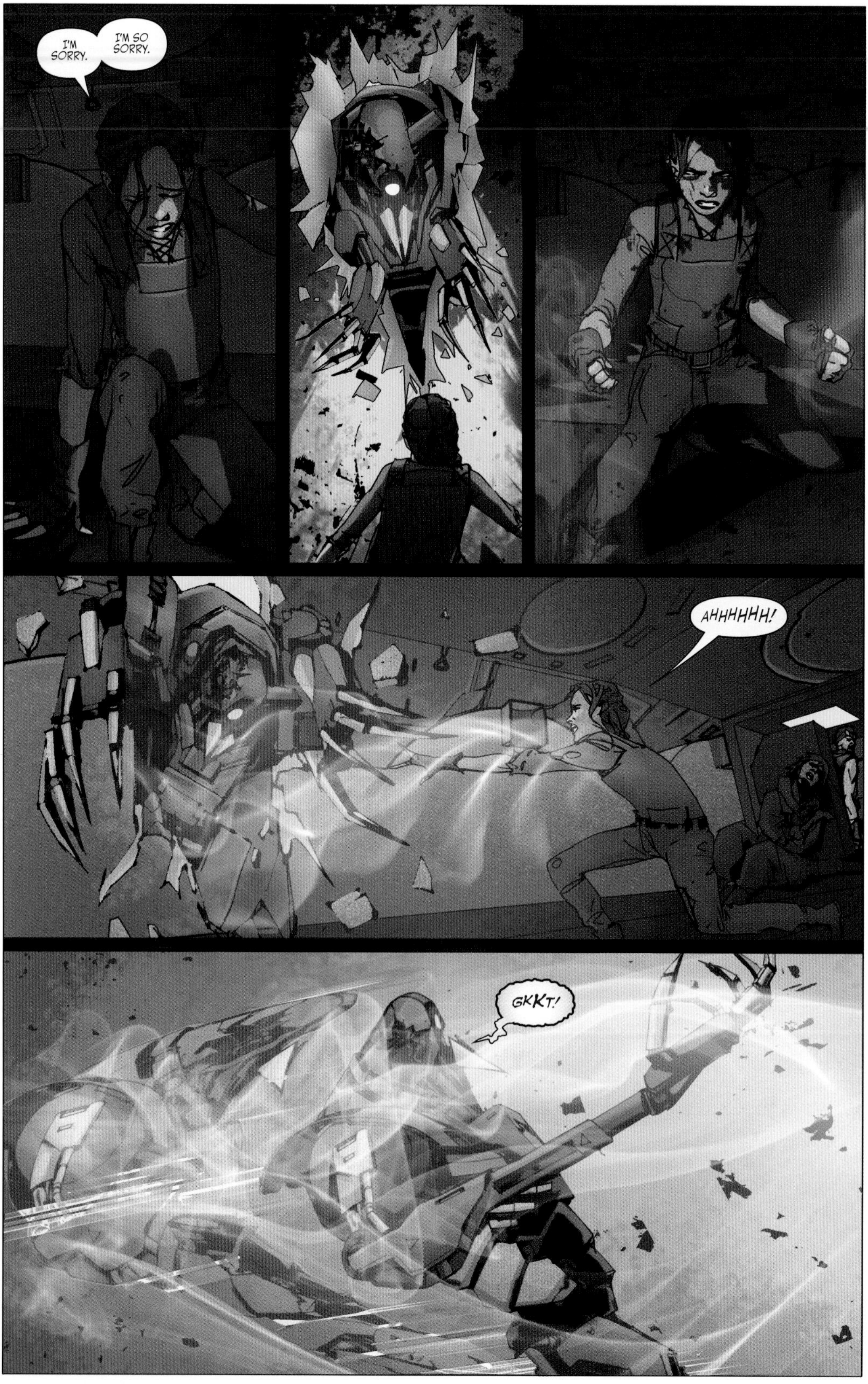
I'M SORRY.
I'M SO SORRY.
AHHHHHH!
GKKT!

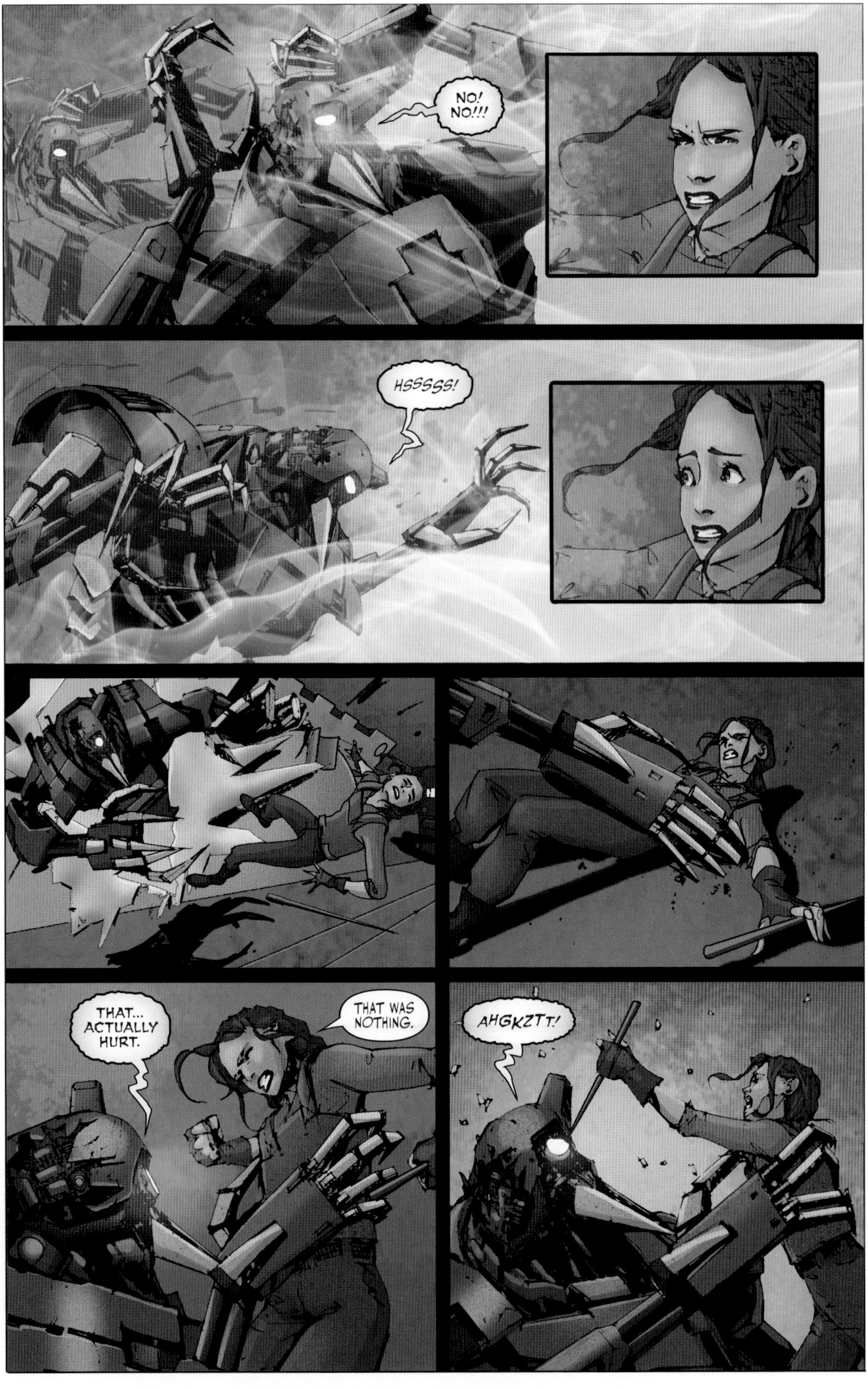
NO! NO!!!
HSSSSS!
THAT... ACTUALLY HURT.
THAT WAS NOTHING.
AHGKZTT!

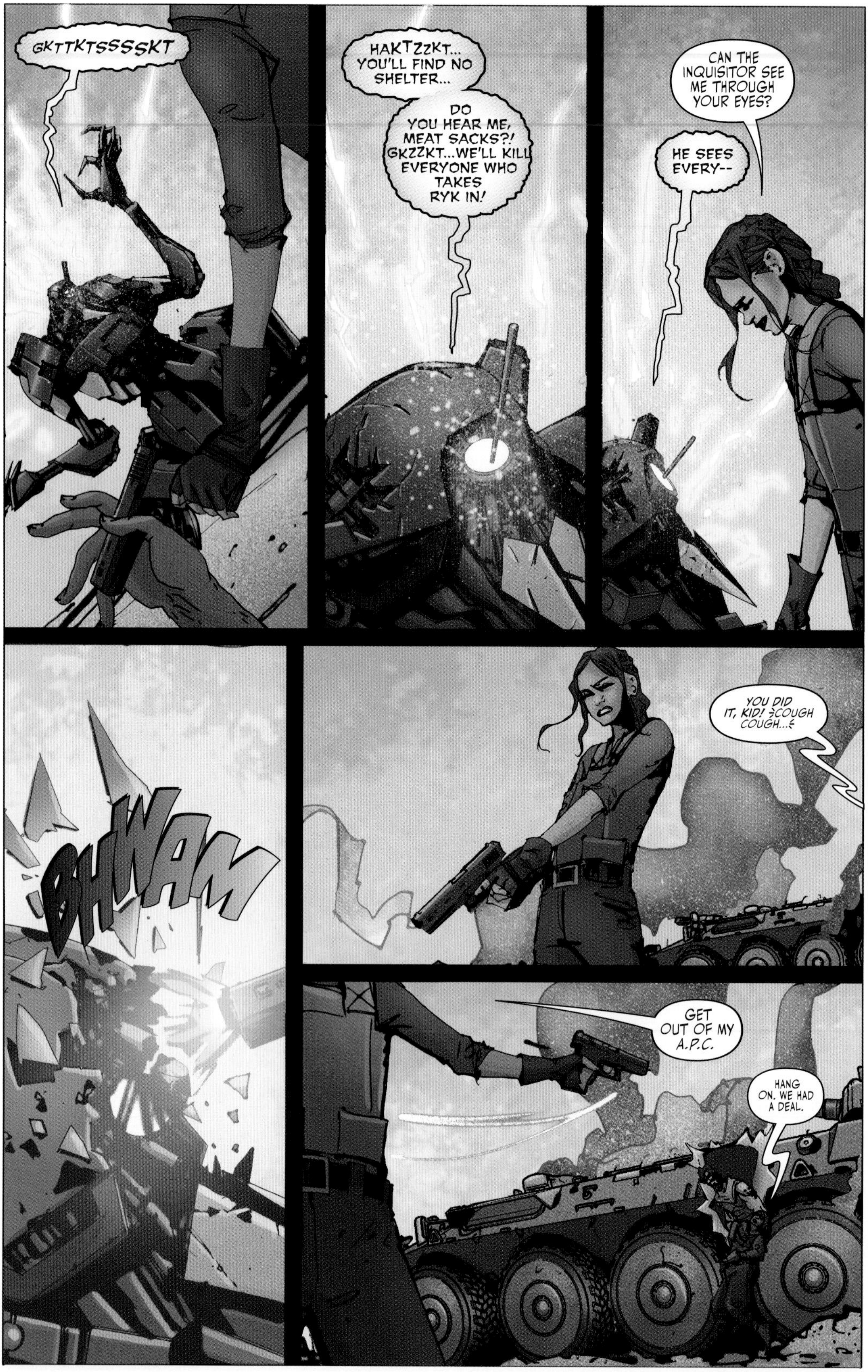
GKTTKTSSSSKT
HAKTZZKT... YOU'LL FIND NO SHELTER...
DO YOU HEAR ME, MEAT SACKS?! GKZZKT...WE'LL KILL EVERYONE WHO TAKES RYK IN!
CAN THE INQUISITOR SEE ME THROUGH YOUR EYES?
HE SEES EVERY--
BHWAM
YOU DID IT, KID! ⋟COUGH COUGH...⋞
GET OUT OF MY A.P.C.
HANG ON. WE HAD A DEAL.

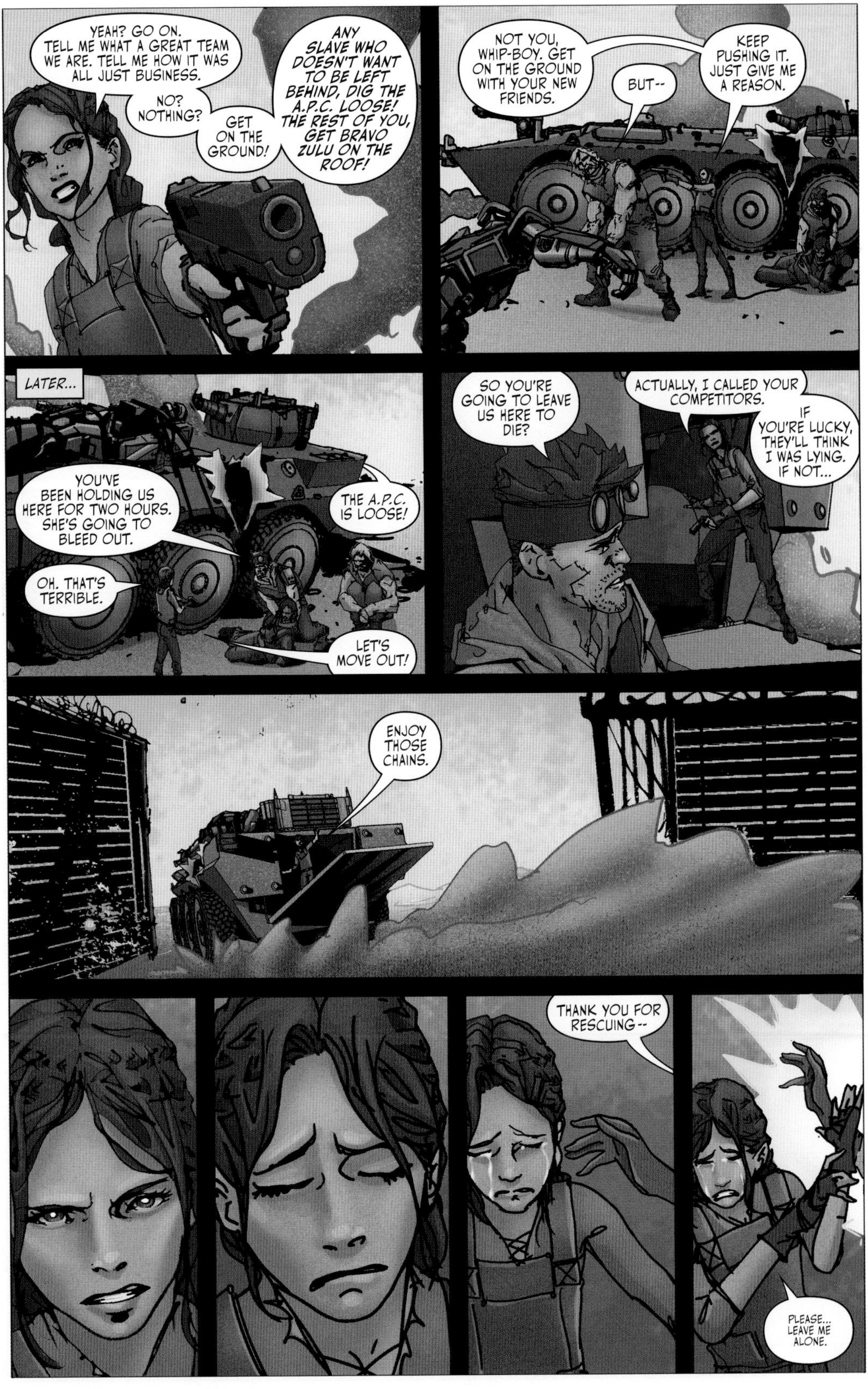
YEAH? GO ON. TELL ME WHAT A GREAT TEAM WE ARE. TELL ME HOW IT WAS ALL JUST BUSINESS.
NO? NOTHING?
GET ON THE GROUND!
ANY SLAVE WHO DOESN'T WANT TO BE LEFT BEHIND, DIG THE A.P.C. LOOSE! THE REST OF YOU, GET BRAVO ZULU ON THE ROOF!
NOT YOU, WHIP-BOY. GET ON THE GROUND WITH YOUR NEW FRIENDS.
BUT--
KEEP PUSHING IT. JUST GIVE ME A REASON.
LATER...
YOU'VE BEEN HOLDING US HERE FOR TWO HOURS. SHE'S GOING TO BLEED OUT.
OH. THAT'S TERRIBLE.
THE A.P.C. IS LOOSE!
LET'S MOVE OUT!
SO YOU'RE GOING TO LEAVE US HERE TO DIE?
ACTUALLY, I CALLED YOUR COMPETITORS.
IF YOU'RE LUCKY, THEY'LL THINK I WAS LYING. IF NOT...
ENJOY THOSE CHAINS.
THANK YOU FOR RESCUING--
PLEASE... LEAVE ME ALONE.

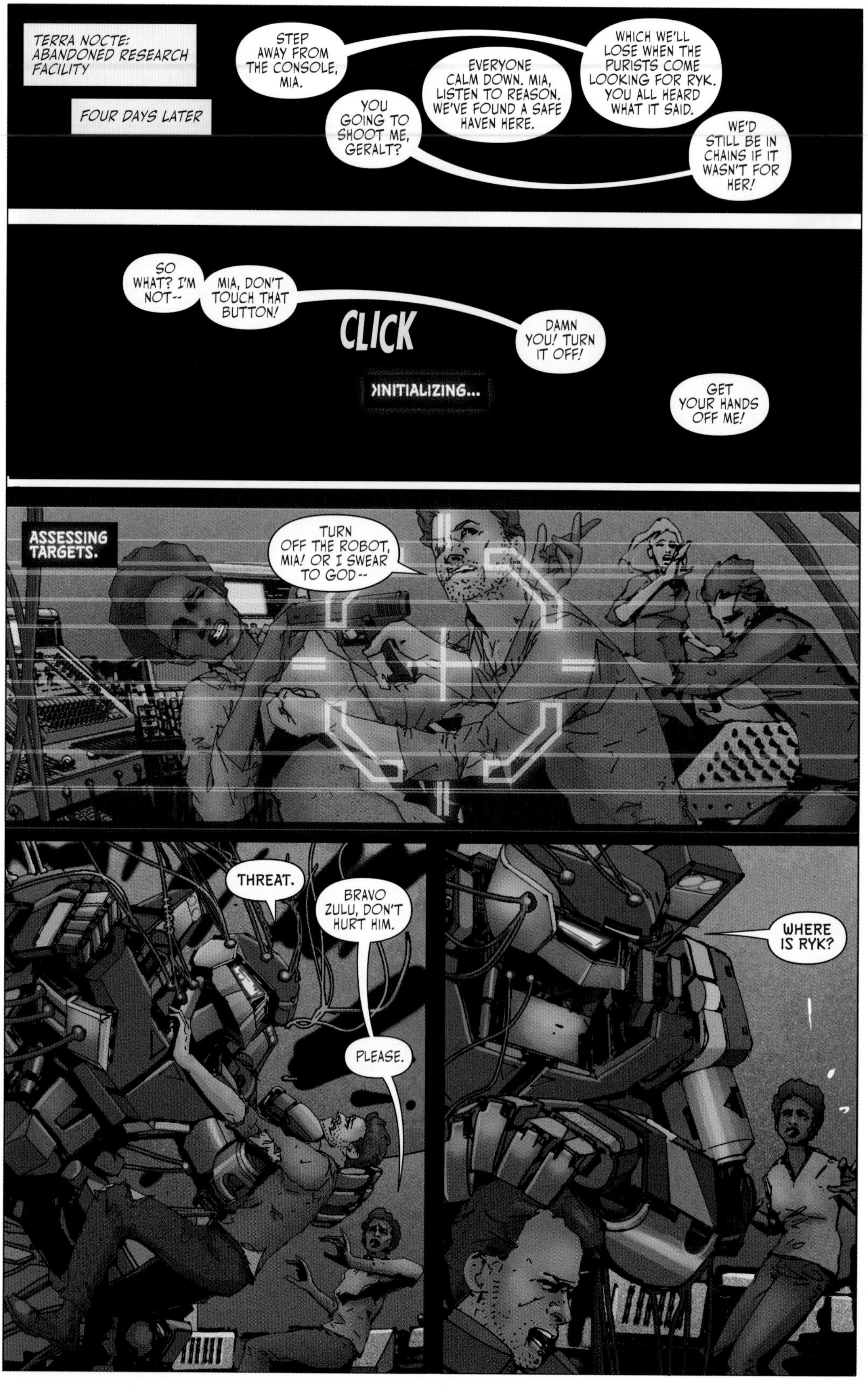

TERRA NOCTE: ABANDONED RESEARCH FACILITY
FOUR DAYS LATER
STEP AWAY FROM THE CONSOLE, MIA.
YOU GOING TO SHOOT ME, GERALT?
EVERYONE CALM DOWN. MIA, LISTEN TO REASON. WE'VE FOUND A SAFE HAVEN HERE.
WHICH WE'LL LOSE WHEN THE PURISTS COME LOOKING FOR RYK. YOU ALL HEARD WHAT IT SAID.
WE'D STILL BE IN CHAINS IF IT WASN'T FOR HER!
SO WHAT? I'M NOT--
MIA, DON'T TOUCH THAT BUTTON!
CLICK
DAMN YOU! TURN IT OFF!
>INITIALIZING...
GET YOUR HANDS OFF ME!
ASSESSING TARGETS.
TURN OFF THE ROBOT, MIA! OR I SWEAR TO GOD--
THREAT.
BRAVO ZULU, DON'T HURT HIM.
PLEASE.
WHERE IS RYK?

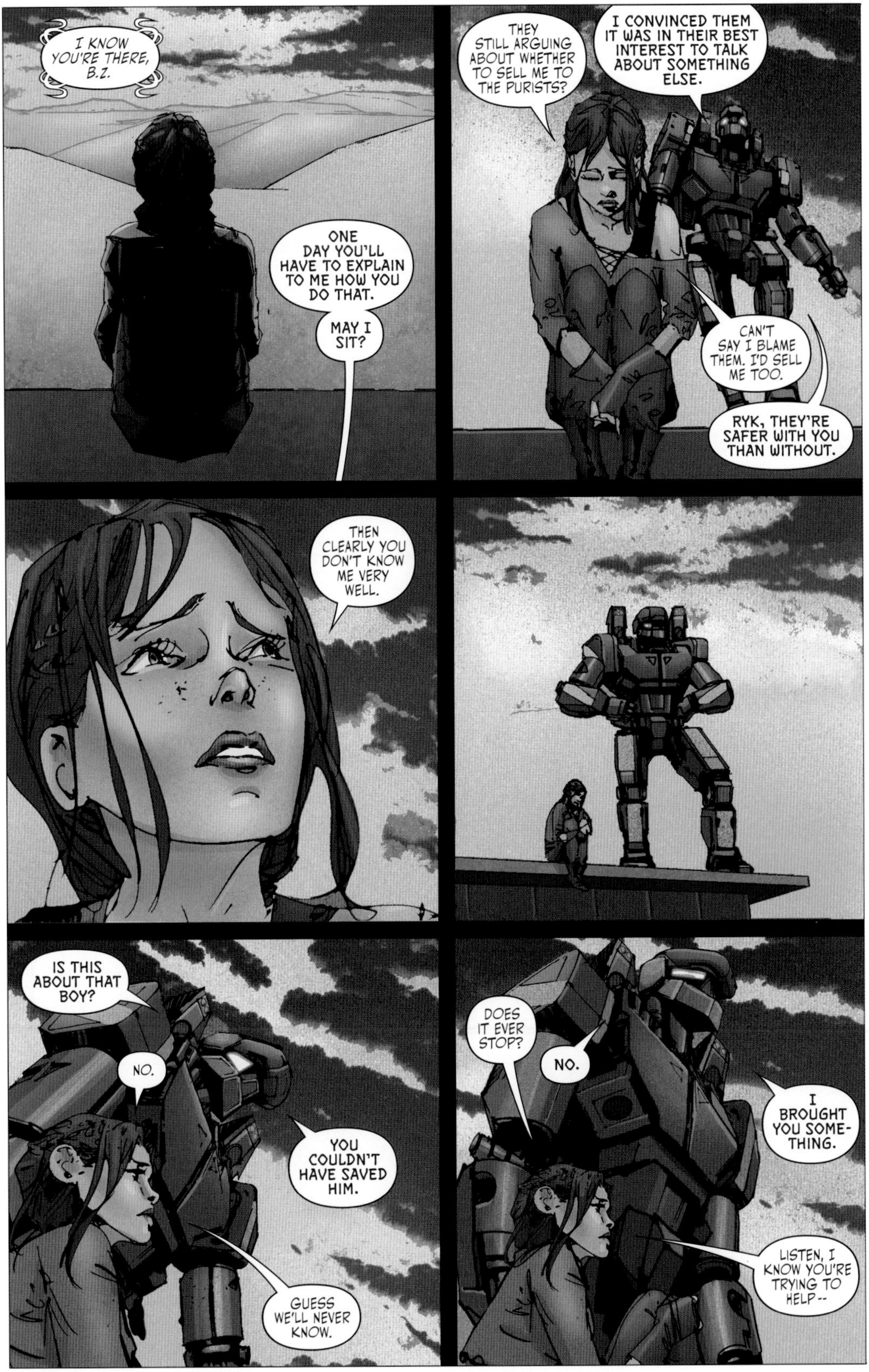
I KNOW YOU'RE THERE, B.Z.
ONE DAY YOU'LL HAVE TO EXPLAIN TO ME HOW YOU DO THAT.
MAY I SIT?
THEY STILL ARGUING ABOUT WHETHER TO SELL ME TO THE PURISTS?
I CONVINCED THEM IT WAS IN THEIR BEST INTEREST TO TALK ABOUT SOMETHING ELSE.
CAN'T SAY I BLAME THEM. I'D SELL ME TOO.
RYK, THEY'RE SAFER WITH YOU THAN WITHOUT.
THEN CLEARLY YOU DON'T KNOW ME VERY WELL.
IS THIS ABOUT THAT BOY?
NO.
YOU COULDN'T HAVE SAVED HIM.
GUESS WE'LL NEVER KNOW.
DOES IT EVER STOP?
NO.
I BROUGHT YOU SOME-THING.
LISTEN, I KNOW YOU'RE TRYING TO HELP--

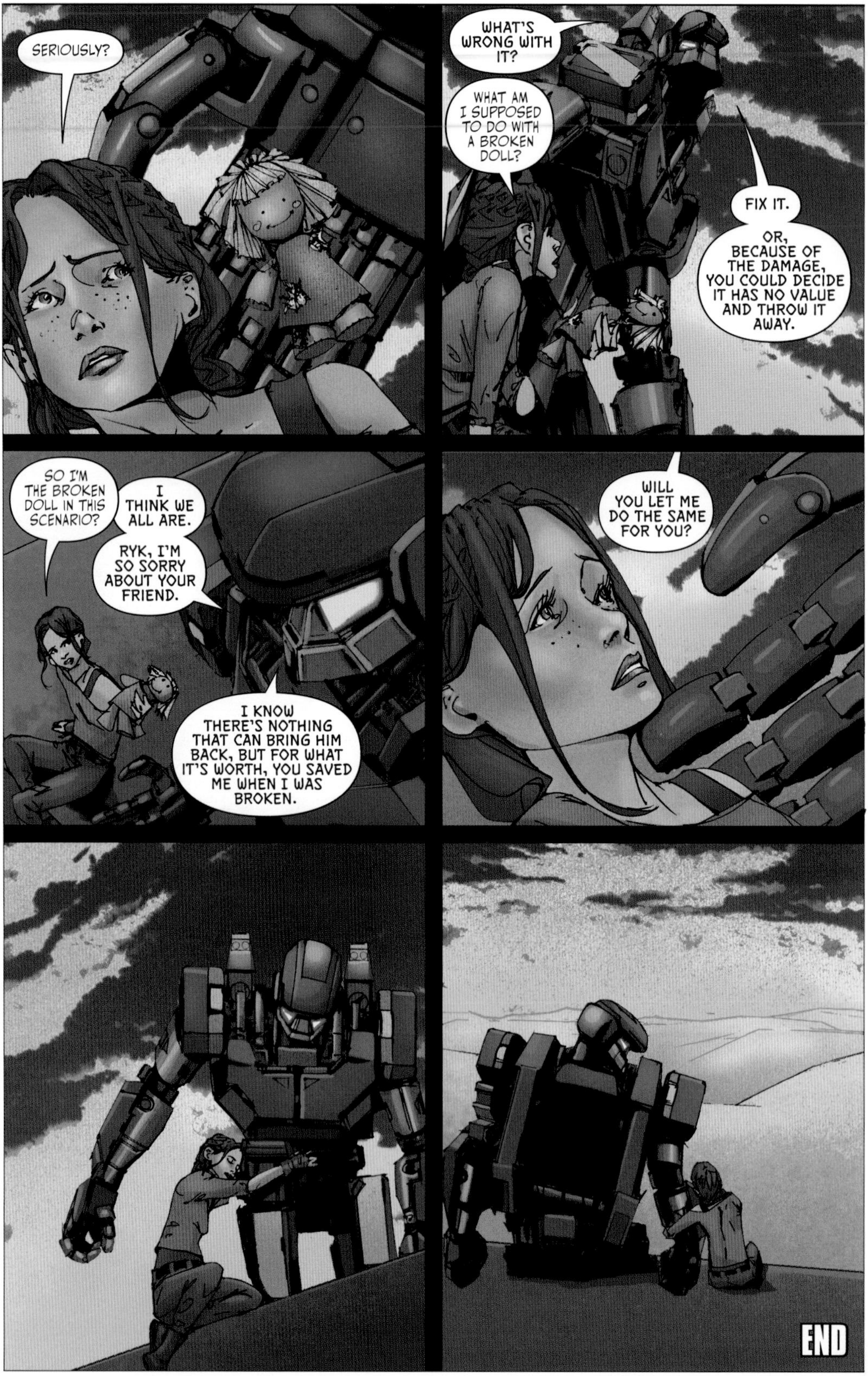
SERIOUSLY?
WHAT'S WRONG WITH IT?
WHAT AM I SUPPOSED TO DO WITH A BROKEN DOLL?
FIX IT.
OR, BECAUSE OF THE DAMAGE, YOU COULD DECIDE IT HAS NO VALUE AND THROW IT AWAY.
SO I'M THE BROKEN DOLL IN THIS SCENARIO?
I THINK WE ALL ARE.
RYK, I'M SO SORRY ABOUT YOUR FRIEND.
I KNOW THERE'S NOTHING THAT CAN BRING HIM BACK, BUT FOR WHAT IT'S WORTH, YOU SAVED ME WHEN I WAS BROKEN.
WILL YOU LET ME DO THE SAME FOR YOU?
END

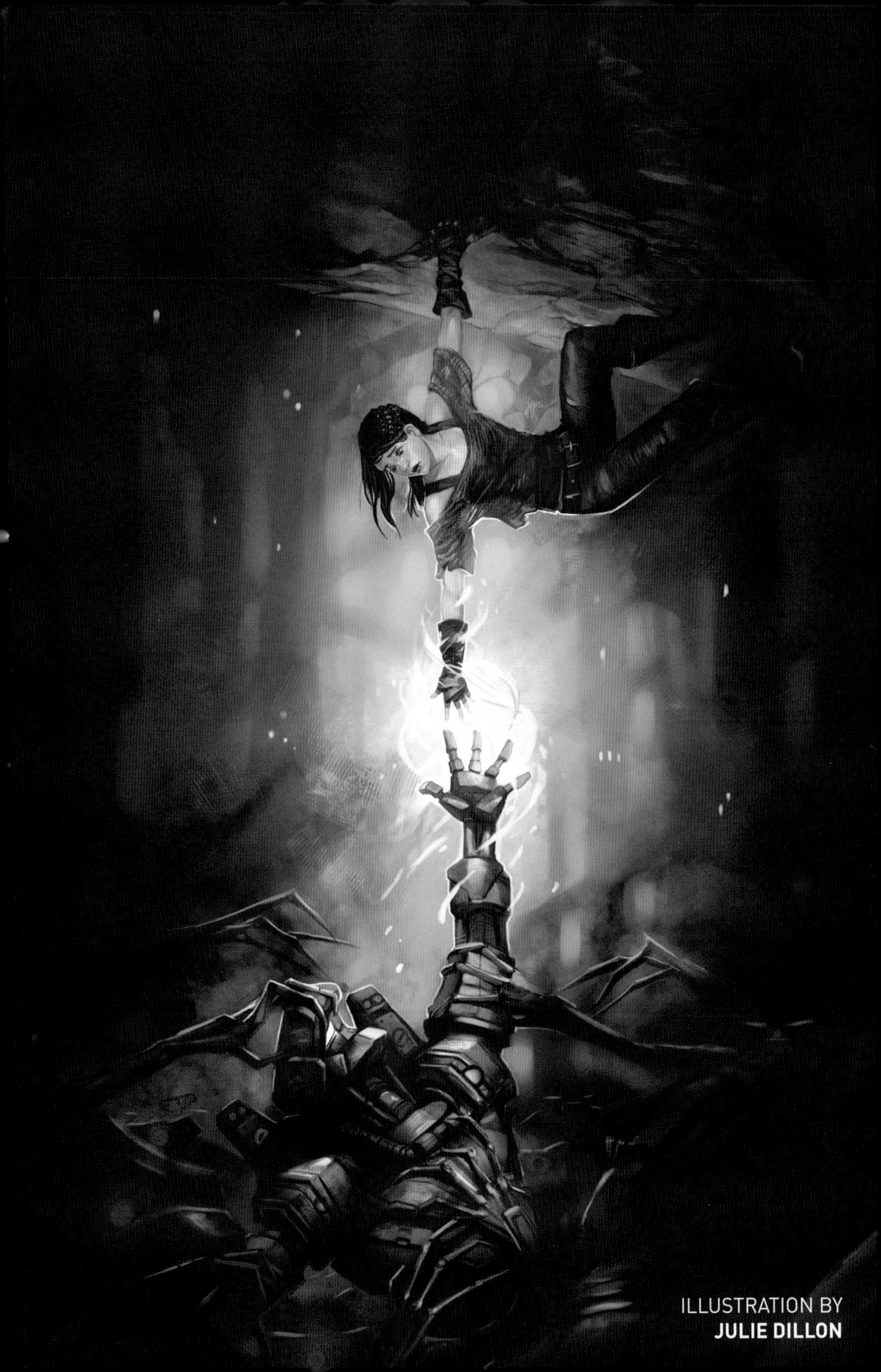

ILLUSTRATION BY
**JULIE DILLON**

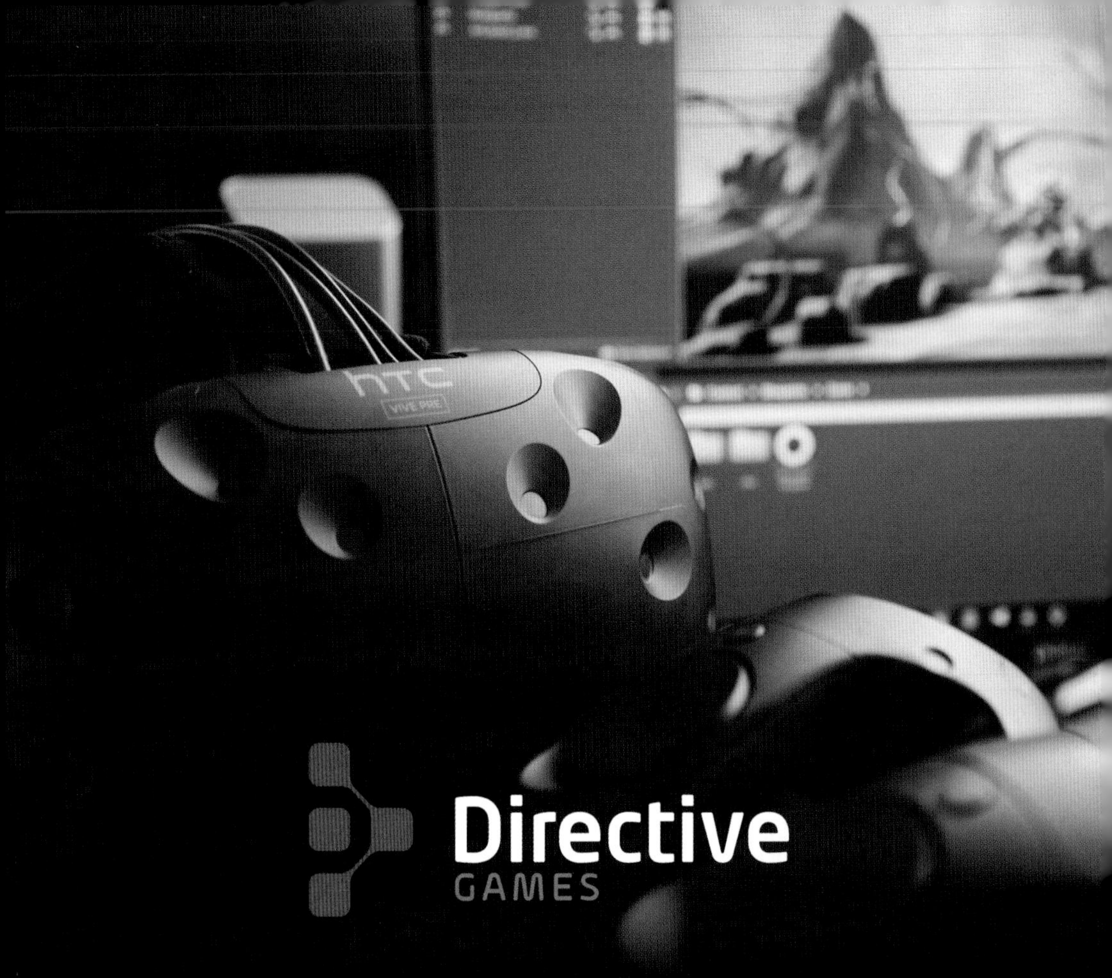
Directive
GAMES

# THE MACHINES

**The Machines** is a strategy game with moba-inspired features where players build an army of robots, and duke it out in PVP both in VR and on mobile.

The game is one of the first cross-platform VR / mobile games created.

 iOS

 Daydream

VIVE

 oculus

 Directive GAMES